Town of Pelham Ontario in Colour Photos, Saving Our History One Photo at a Time

Photography
by Barbara Raué
2018

Series Name:
Cruising Ontario

Book 196: Fenwick, Ridgeville, Fonthill, Pelham

Cover photo: 840 Canboro Road, Fenwick, Page 22

Series Name: Cruising Ontario
Saving Our History One Photo at a Time
in colour photos

Books Available in Alphabetical Order:
Aberfoyle, Acton, Alton, Amherstburg, Ancaster, Arthur, Aylmer, Ayr, Belleville, Bloomingdale, Brantford, Brockville, Burford, Burlington, Caledon, Caledonia, Cambridge, Clifford, Conestogo, Delhi, Dorchester to Aylmer, Drayton, Drumbo, Dundas, Eden Mills, Elmira, Elora, Erin, Essex, Fergus, Goderich, Guelph, Hagersville, Hamilton, Hanover, Harriston, Hespeler, Jarvis, Kingston, Kingsville, Kitchener, Lake Superior, Linwood, Listowel, London, Lucknow, Merrickville, Mono, Mount Forest, Neustadt, New Hamburg, Newboro, Niagara-on-the-Lake, Oakville, Orangeville, Orillia, Owen Sound, Palmerston, Paris, Perth, Peterborough, Petrolia, Port Colborne, Port Elgin, Portland, Preston, Rockwood, Sarnia, Sault Ste. Marie, Seaforth, Sheffield, Shelburne, Simcoe, Smiths Falls, Southampton, St. George, St. Jacobs, St. Marys, St. Thomas, Stoney Creek, Stratford, Thamesford, Thunder Bay, Tillsonburg, Waterdown, Waterford, Waterloo, Welland, Wellesley, Westport, Windsor, Wingham, Woodstock

Book 184: Mt Pleasant, Onondaga, Newport
Book 185-186: Grimsby
Book 187: Toronto
Book 188: Collingwood
Book 189-193: St. Catharines
Book 194: Smithville
Book 195: Town of Lincoln
Book 196: Town of Pelham

Other Books by Barbara Raue

Coins of Gold

Arrows, Indians and Love

The Life and Times of Barbara

The Cromwell Family Book

Laura Secord Discovered

Daddy Where Are You?

Montana Series
Book 1: Montana Dream
Book 2: Life on the Montana Frontier
Book 3: Montana to Boston and Back
Book 4: Montana Sons Go to War
Book 5: Montana Sons Return From War

Visit Barbara's website to view all of her books
http://barbararaue.ca

Table of Contents

Fenwick	Page 6
Ridgeville	Page 21
Fonthill	Page 26
Pelham	Page 51
Architectural Terms	Page 60
Building Styles	Page 63

Fenwick is a community in the in the town of Pelham located in the Niagara Region. Welland is the closest city center. The community was named in 1853. The name probably comes from Fenwick, East Ayrshire in Scotland, which was the birthplace of Dr. John Fraser, who was reeve of Pelham Township at the time.

Ridgeville is a community within the town of Pelham. It borders the western limit of Fonthill. It derives its name from its location on the south western ridge of the Fonthill Kame. It has a post office, a rural mail route named *Ridgeville*, a small number of shops found along Canboro Road, including a bakery, chocolate shop and specialty home and bath shops, the local high school, Gwennol Organic Blueberry Farm and the Berry Patch Tea Room.

Fonthill is a community in the town of Pelham. It has a few small industries, but is primarily a residential suburb known for its fruit orchards, nature trails, and neighborly attitude.

Fonthill shares its name with the Fonthill Kame, on which it is located, formed by glacial deposits. Effingham Creek, a cold-water stream, originates in the glacial silts and sands of Short Hills area of the moraine, northwest of Fonthill. Effingham Creek is a tributary to Twelve-Mile Creek, which empties into Lake Ontario.

The Fonthill Kame is a geological feature in the form of a large, isolated hill composed of sand and gravel deposited by the retreating glaciers of the last ice age. The Fonthill Kame rises about 75 meters (246 feet) above the surrounding land and is the highest elevation in the region. The kame is 6 kilometres (4 miles) east to west and 3 kilometres (2 miles) north to south. It slopes gradually on the west side, more steeply on the south and east and merges with the Short Hills Provincial Park area of the Niagara Escarpment on the north. The Fonthill Kame influences the climate of Pelham by sheltering it from the winds from the southwest. This provides good growing conditions for fruit crops, including the grape vines that supply the local wine industry. It is also mined for sand and gravel.

Letters written by Henry Giles, a settler who came to the area in 1840, suggest that he chose the name Fonthill because the area looked similar to the area around Fonthill Abbey in England. The village's first post office was established in 1856. On June 10, 2006, Fonthill celebrated its 150th anniversary. The celebration was marked by the opening of the band stand (a replica of the original band stand the existed in the early 1900s), historical displays and a variety of musical and artistic presentations.

On a clear day, the tall buildings of Niagara Falls to the East and the Toronto skyline to the North are clearly visible from a vantage point near Effingham Street and south Tice Road just west of Fonthill. This also allows views of Lake Ontario, Lake Erie, and the skyline of Buffalo.

In 1970, the Town of Pelham unified five historical communities: Fonthill, Ridgeville, Effingham, North Pelham and Fenwick into a single town covering more than one hundred and twenty-six thousand square kilometres. This integration brought together a mix of farming (agriculture) and commercialism.

The Town of Pelham is located in the centre of Niagara Region. The town's southern boundary is formed by the Welland River, a meandering waterway that flows into the Niagara River. To the west is the township of West Lincoln, to the east the city of Welland, and to the north the city of St. Catharines. Pelham Township was part of Welland County since the late 1780s. The Town of Pelham derived its name from Pelham Township which was named by John Graves Simcoe in the 1790s. Simcoe gave names to the Townships of Niagara that were created to provide land for Loyalist refugees, disbanded troops former rangers and others after the British defeat in the Revolutionary War (which ended in 1783). The policy of Simcoe was to adopt township names from England.

Fenwick

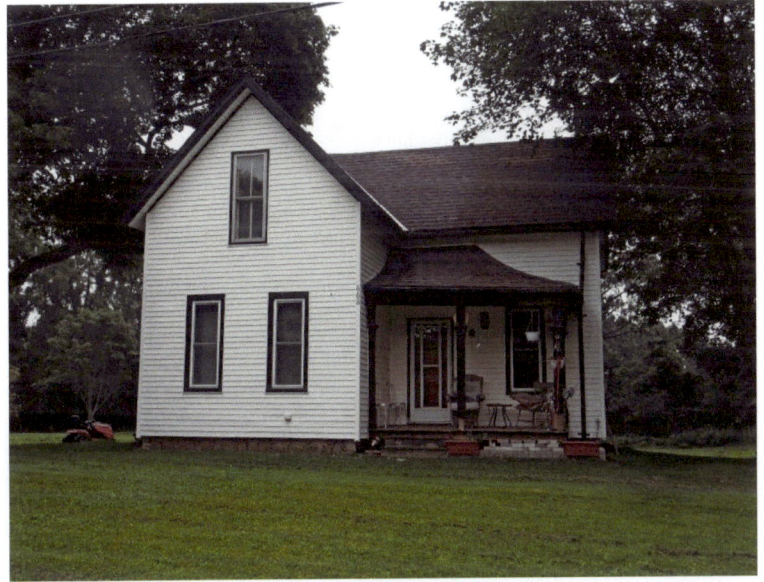

668 Canboro Road

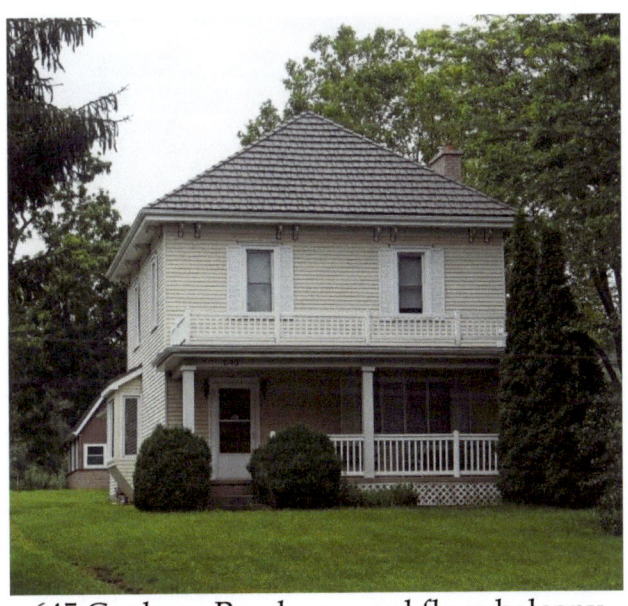

645 Canboro Road – second floor balcony

Fenwick

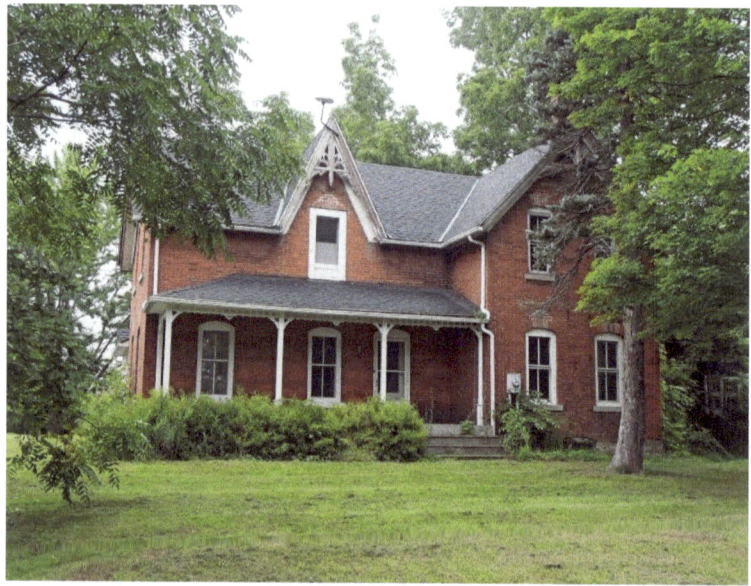

655 Canboro Road – Gothic, verge board trim on gable

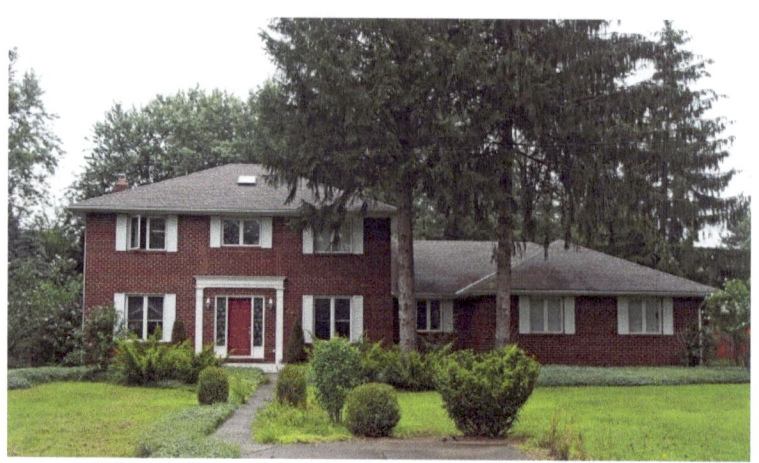

683 Canboro Road – hipped roof, sidelights

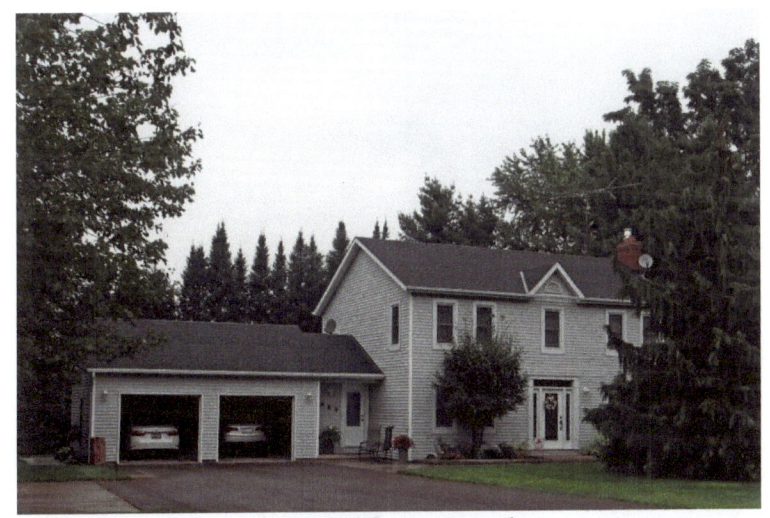

687 Canboro Road

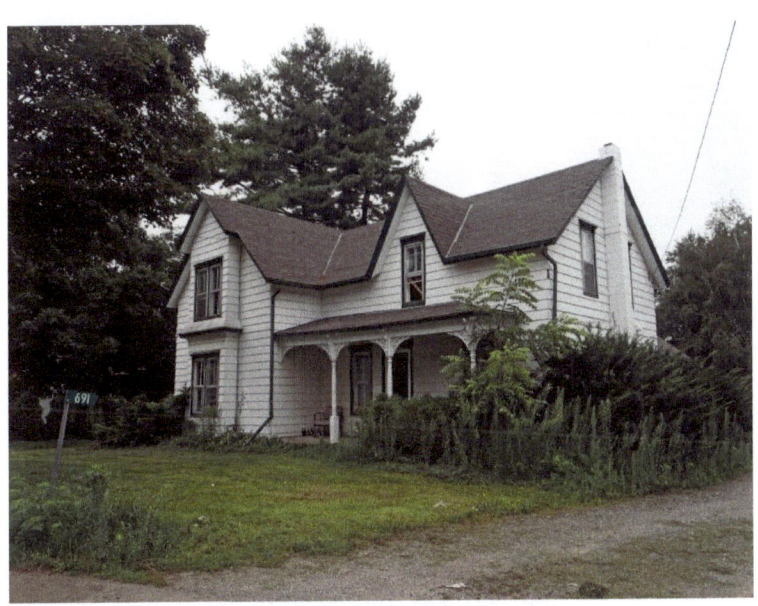

691 Canboro Road - Gothic

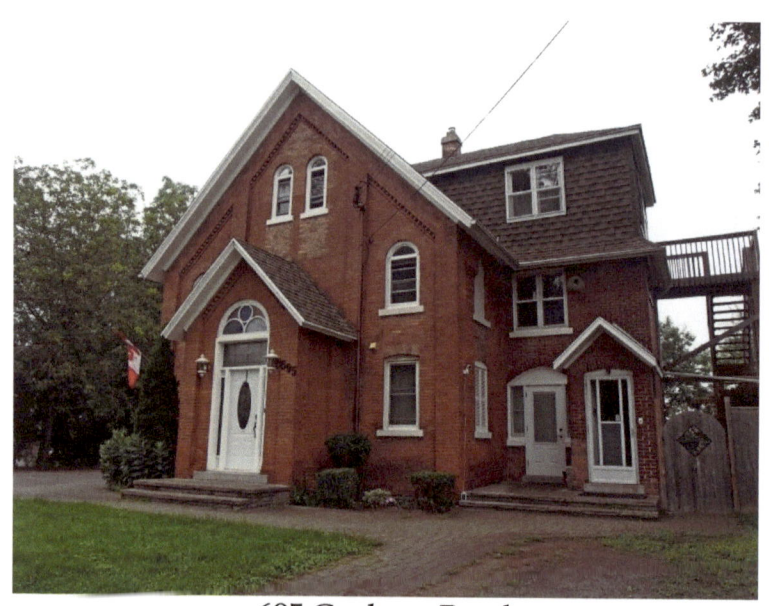

695 Canboro Road

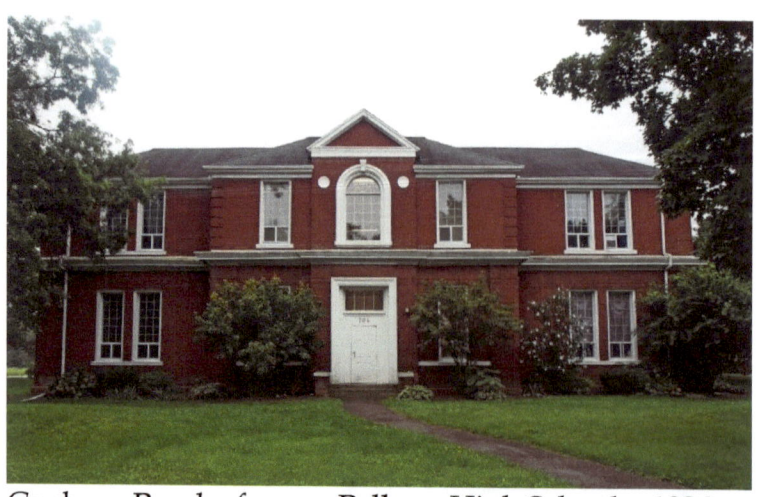

704 Canboro Road – former Pelham High School – 1926 – now Canboro Gardens

Fenwick

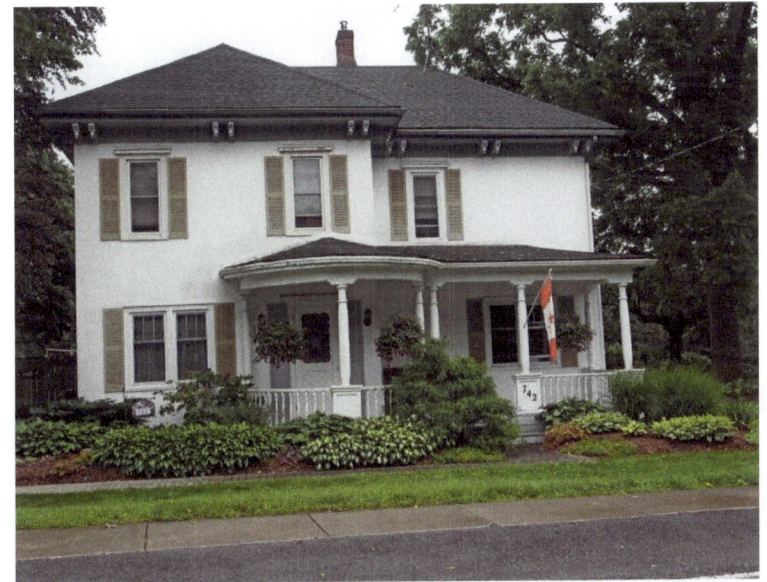

742 Canboro Road – hipped roof, paired cornice brackets

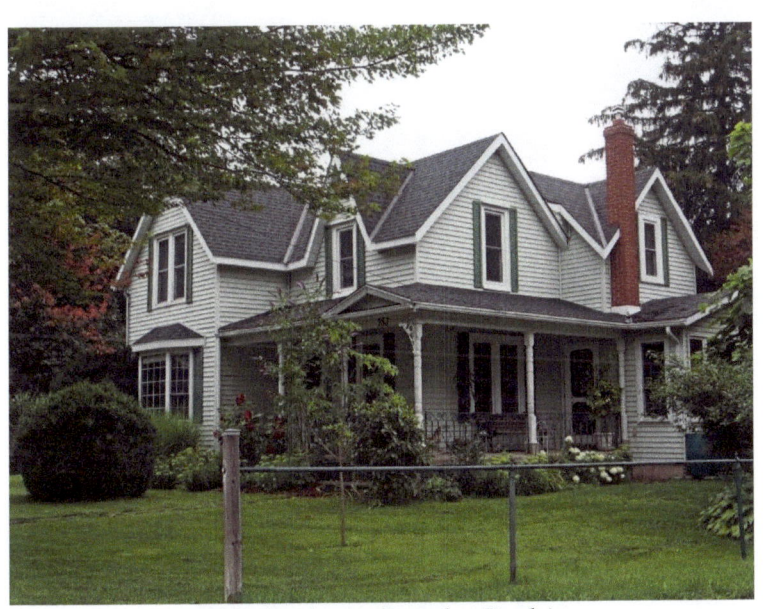

753 Canboro Road - Gothic

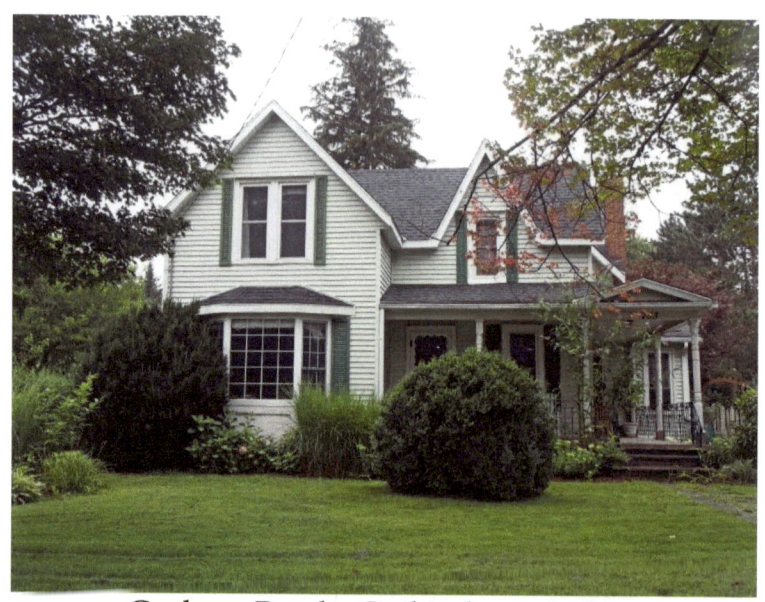
Canboro Road – Gothic, bay window

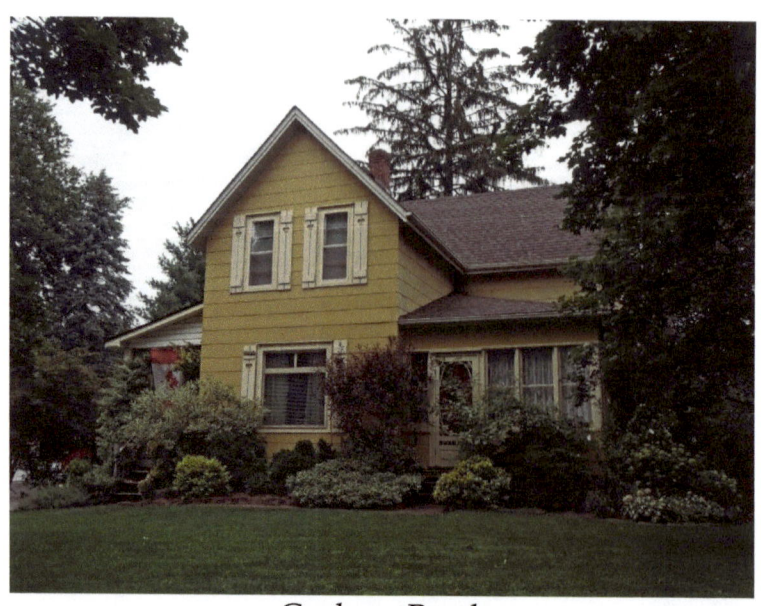
Canboro Road

Fenwick

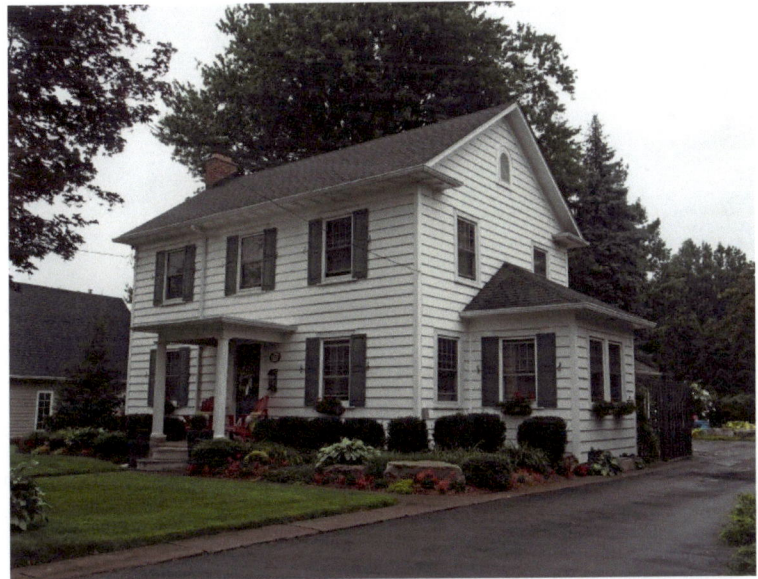

759 Canboro Road – cornice return on end gable, balanced façade

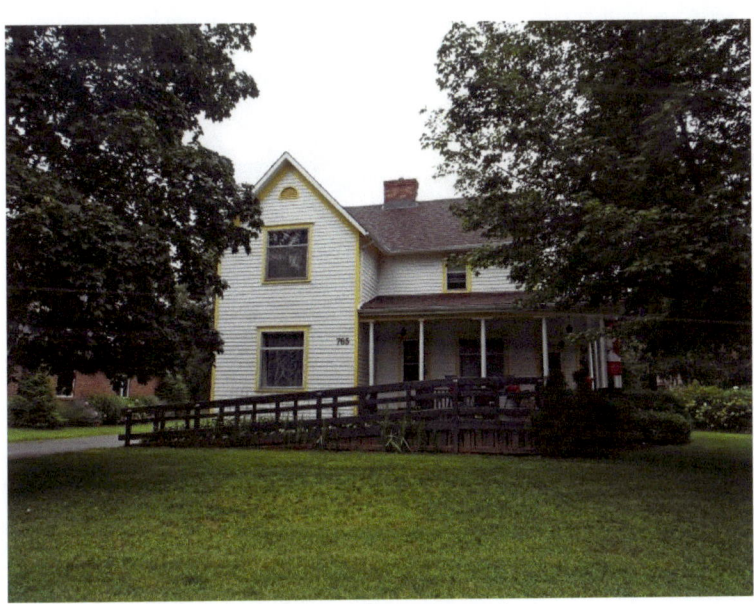

765 Canboro Road

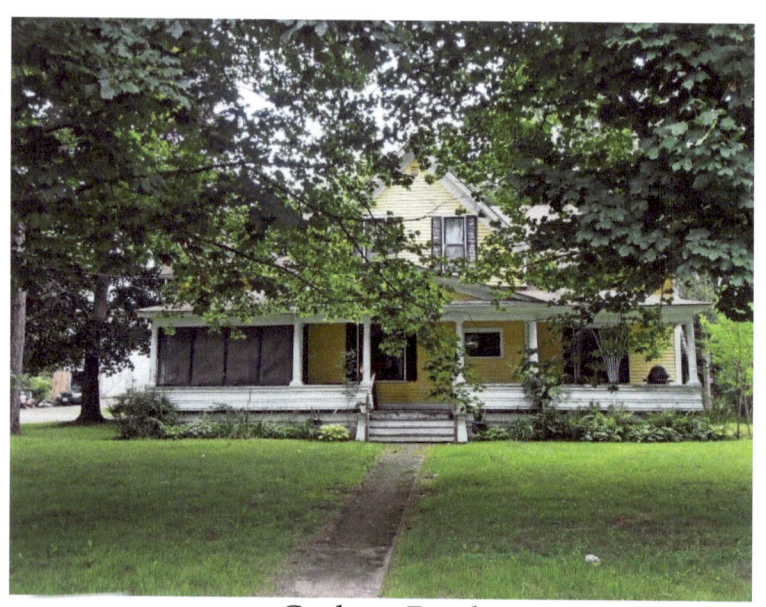

Canboro Road

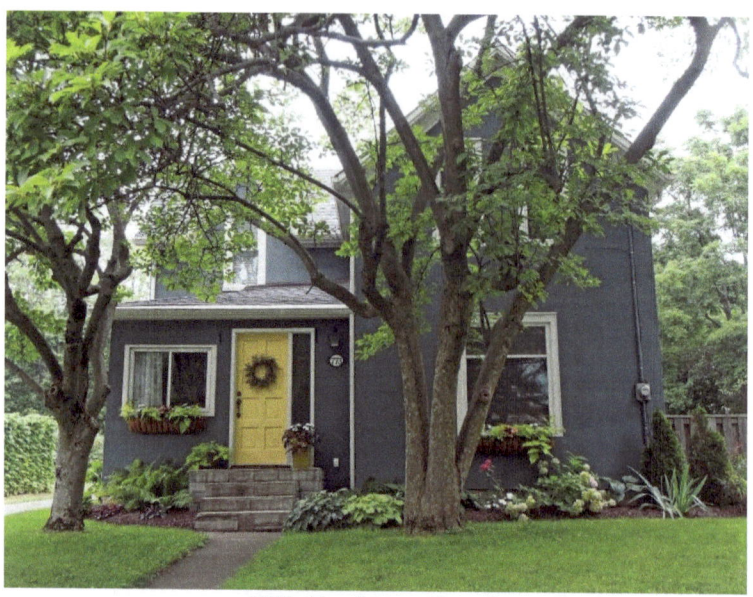

773 Canboro Road

Fenwick

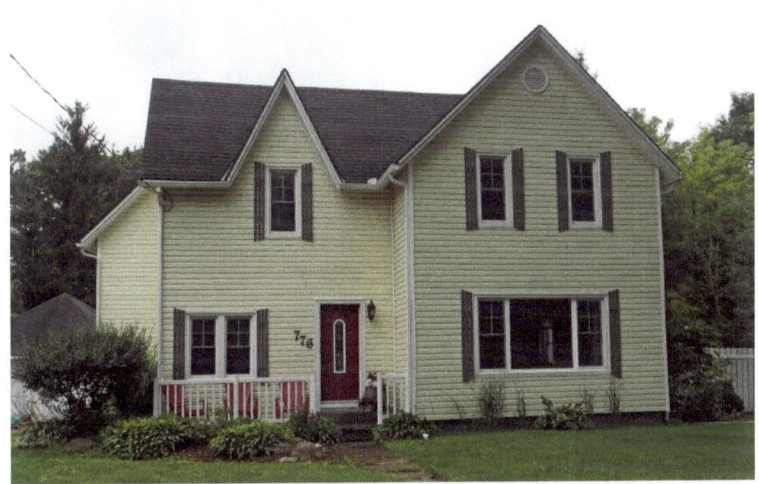

776 Canboro Road - Gothic

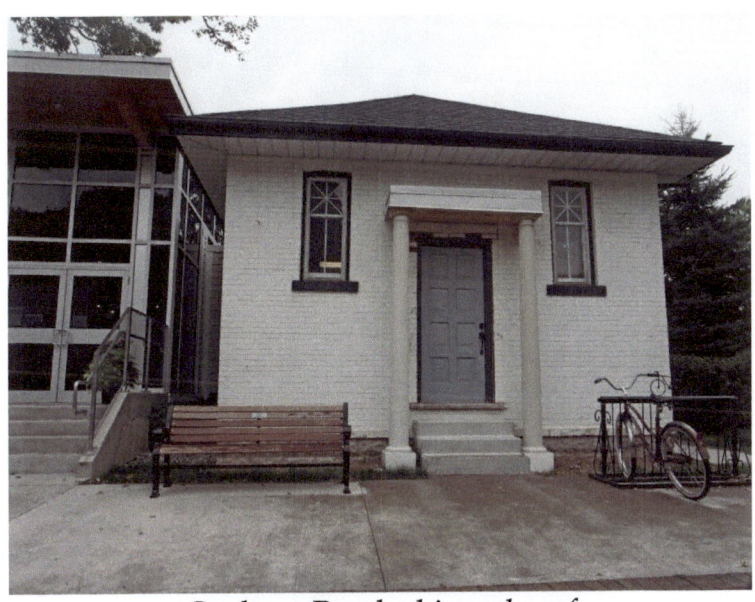

Canboro Road – hipped roof

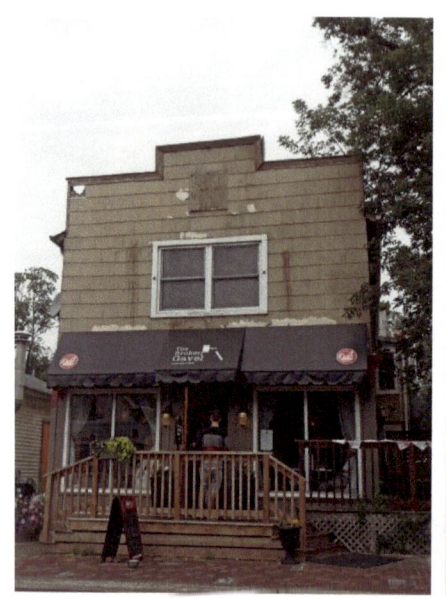 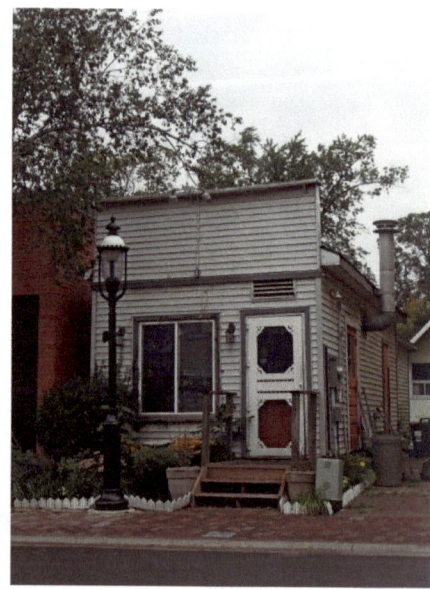

Canboro Road
The Broken Gavel – stepped parapet

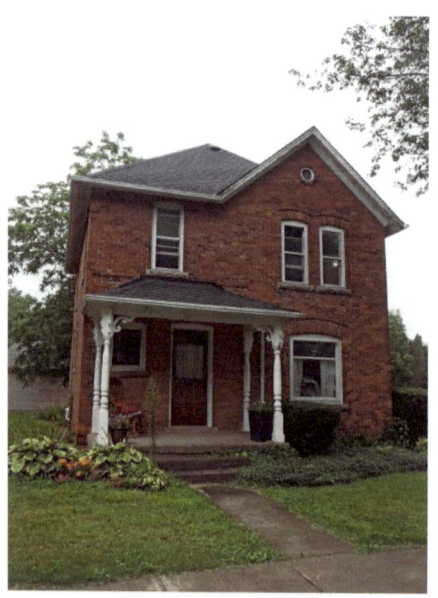

Canboro Road

Fenwick

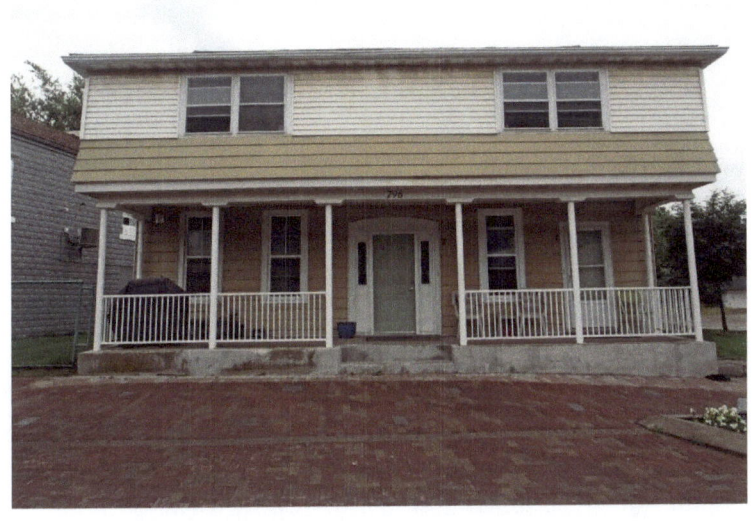

796 Canboro Road – Diffin's Inn

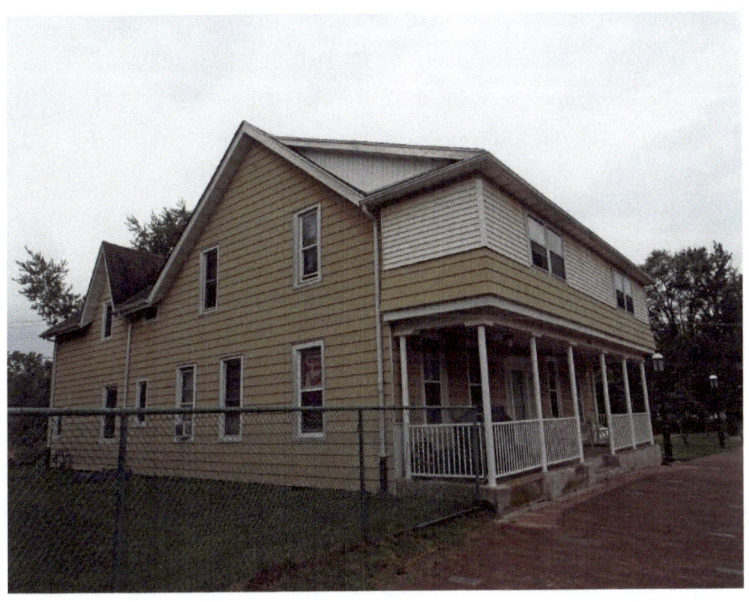

In 1845 two enterprising brothers, Benjamin and George Diffin, built two inns on the Canboro Road or "Great West" Road, near the corner of present day Church Street. It was a time when inns were necessary and as numerous as gas stations are today, and the Canboro Road was a major Niagara route. The small settlement in west Pelham became known as Diffin's Corners. Eight years later, in 1853, the first post office was opened, and the name Fenwick was chosen to honor Dr. Frazer, who was born in Fenwick, Scotland. He became Reeve of Pelham, Warden of Welland County and an M.P.

The two inns were primarily rooming places with stables, but were also taverns. Following the Canada Temperance Act of 1879 there was pressure by temperance organizations to have Welland county implement the Act. It was an optional local measure, prohibiting the sale of intoxicating beverages. Pelham was a temperance stronghold and in the voting on November 10, 1881, the township voted in support of the Act, as did Thorold, the only two municipalities in the region to do so. It was some ninety years later (1971), before liquor was sold again in Pelham.

One of the inns was a frame cottage, later covered with stucco. The one storey veranda, an almost universal addition to houses in Upper Canada and Canada West at the time, is supported by simple posts of classical columns. The other inn became an apartment building.

Fenwick

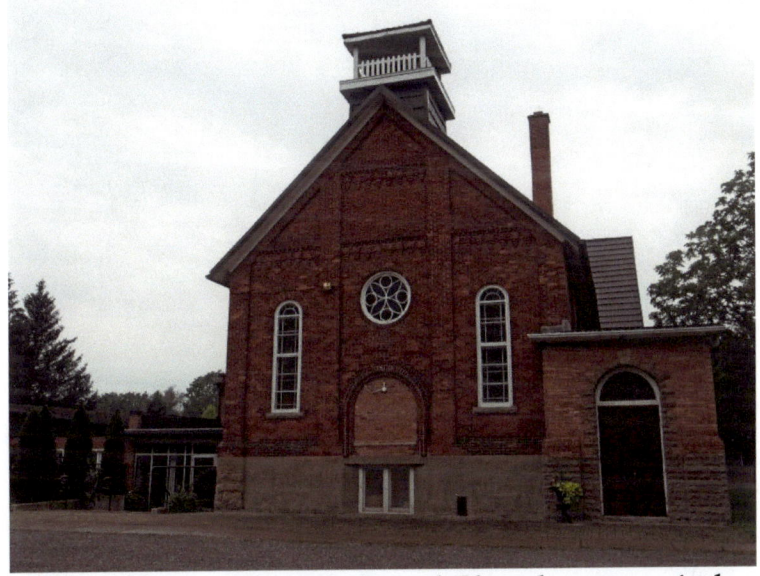

Canboro Road – Fenwick United Church – rose window, cupola on roof

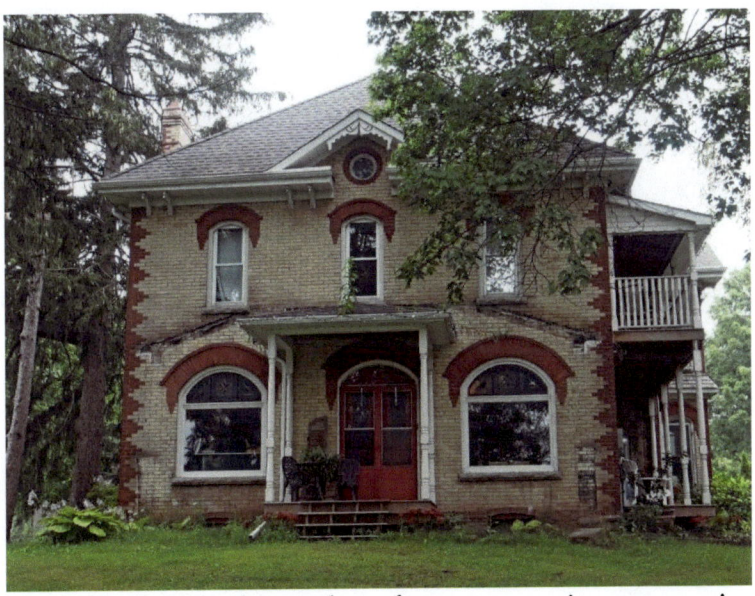

Canboro Road – hipped roof, corner quoins, voussoirs

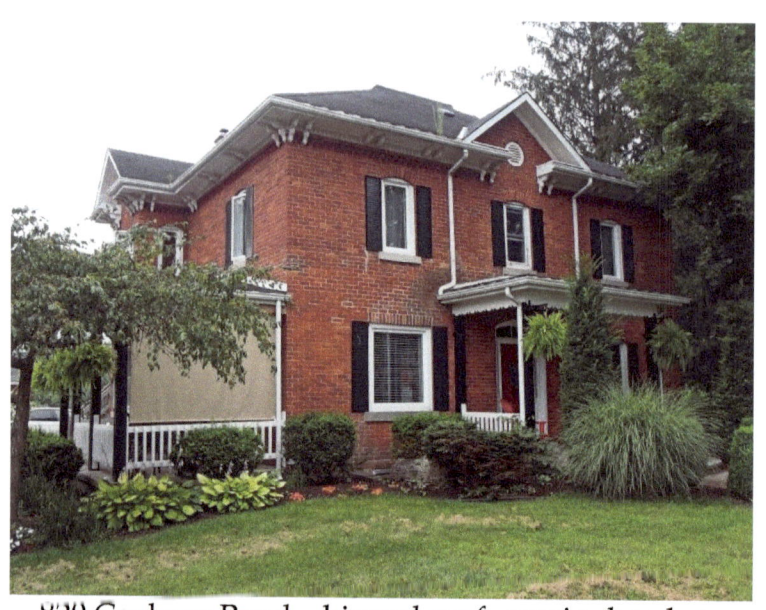
820 Canboro Road – hipped roof, cornice brackets

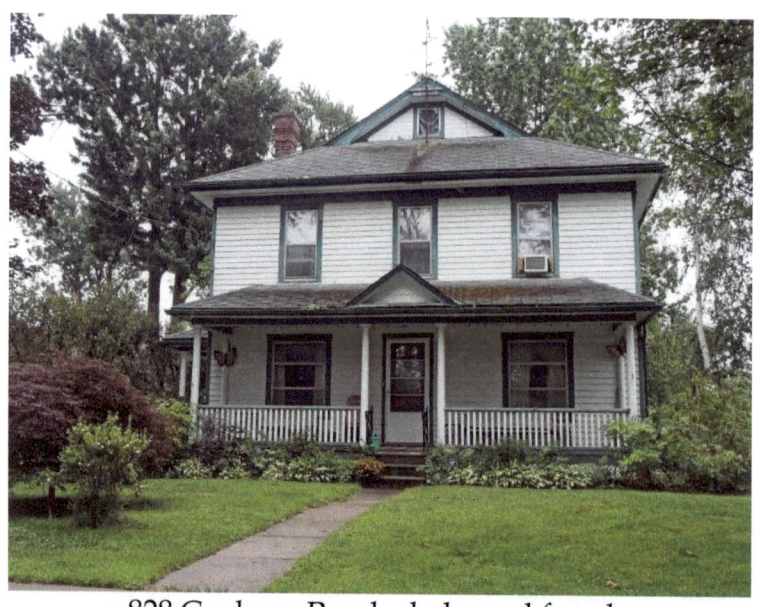
828 Canboro Road – balanced façade

Fenwick

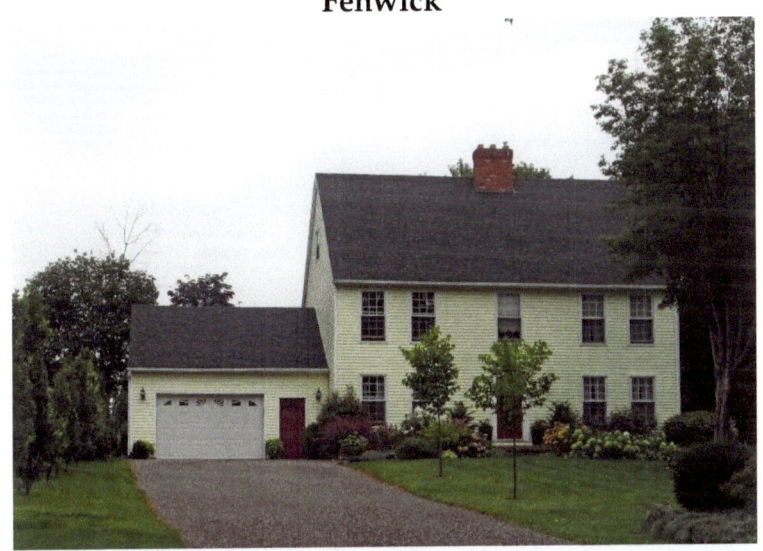

Canboro Road – Georgian, balanced façade, multi-paned windows

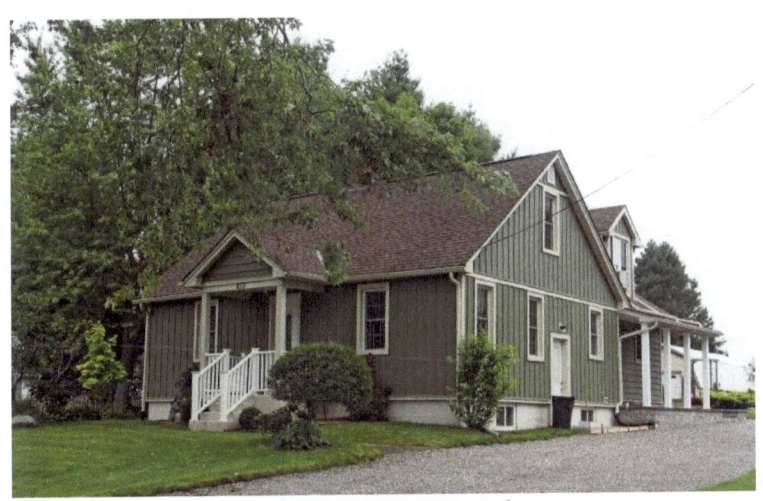

833 Canboro Road

Fenwick

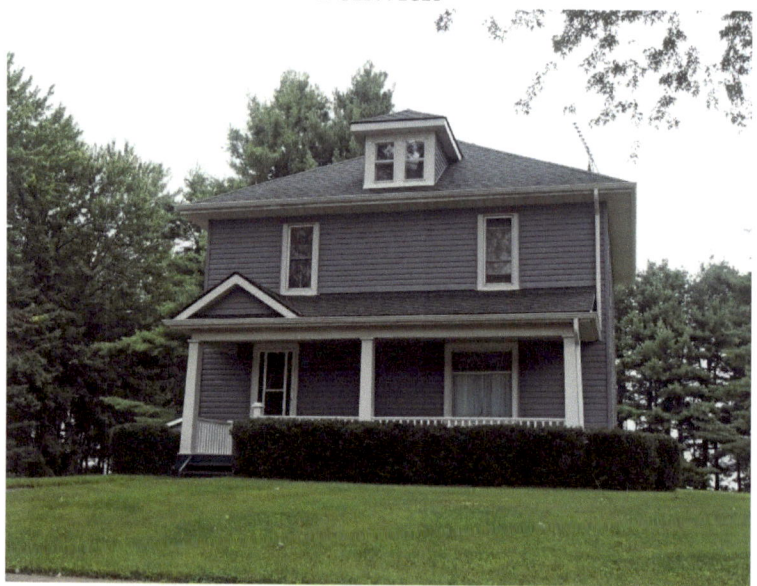

837 Canboro Road - dormer

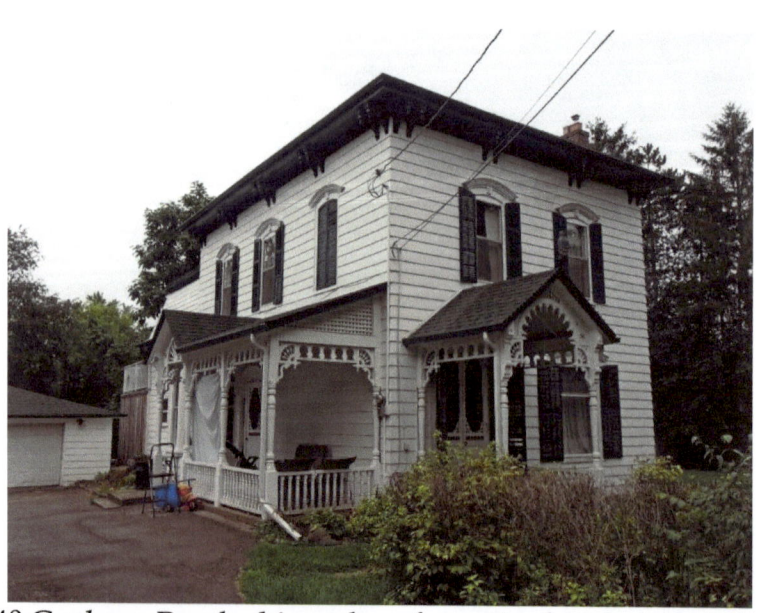

840 Canboro Road – hipped roof, cornice brackets, porches decorated with bric-a-brac

Ridgeville

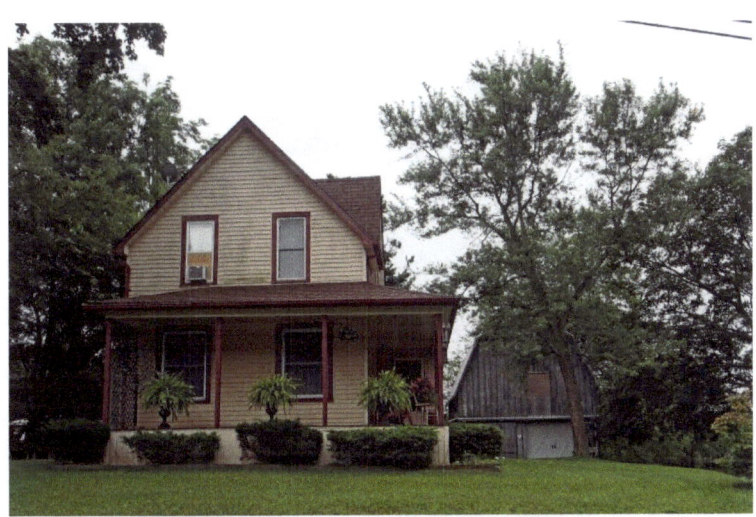

260 Canboro Road - Gothic

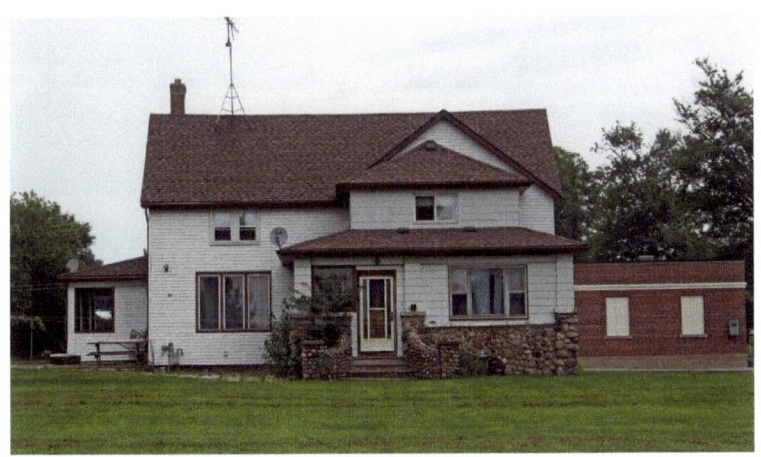

Canboro Road

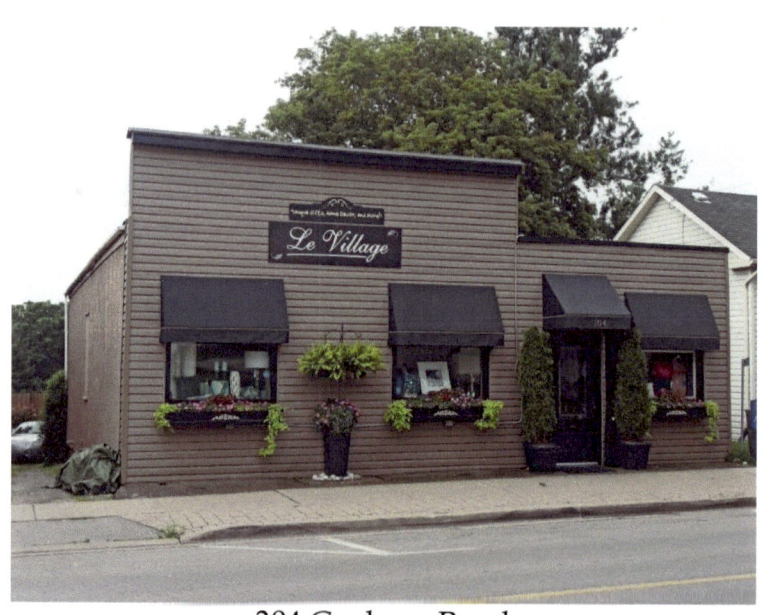

304 Canboro Road

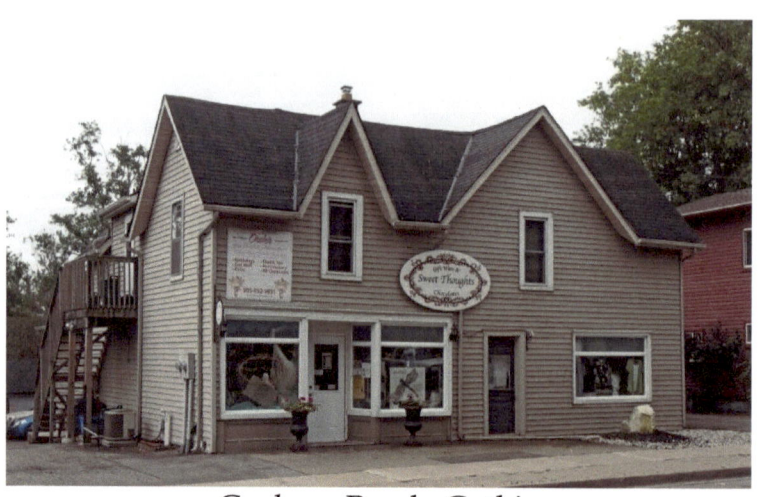

Canboro Road - Gothic

Ridgeville

306 Canboro Road

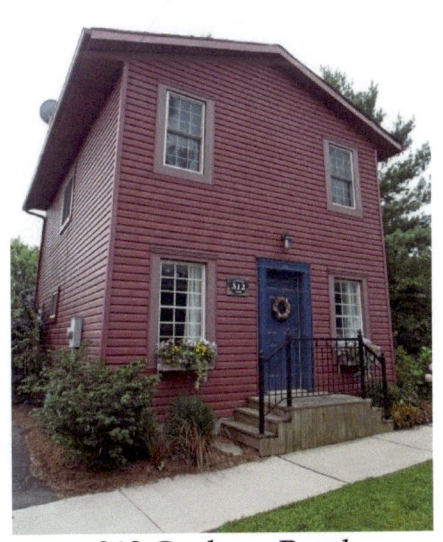

312 Canboro Road

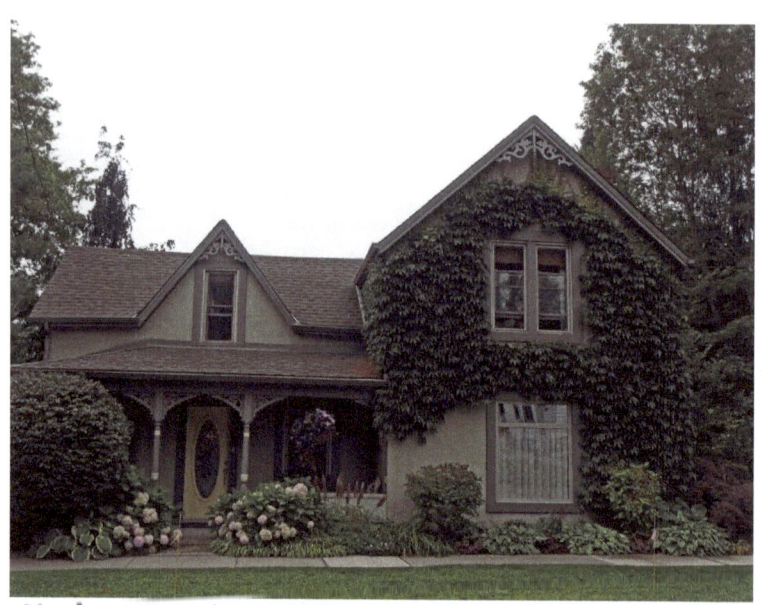

Canboro Road – Gothic – verge board trim on gables

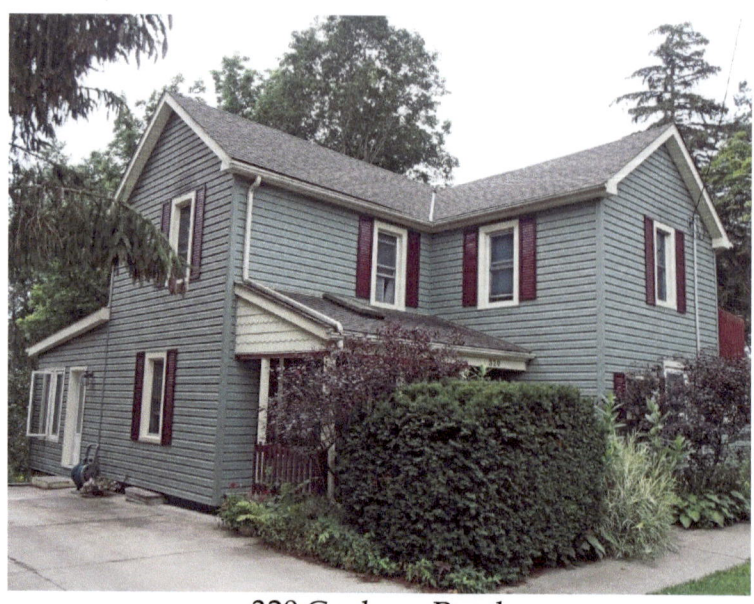

320 Canboro Road

Ridgeville

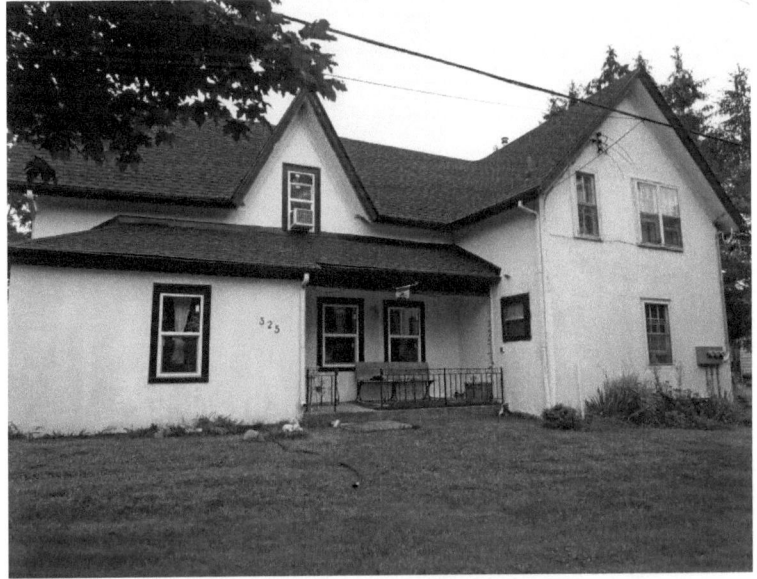

325 Canboro Road - Gothic

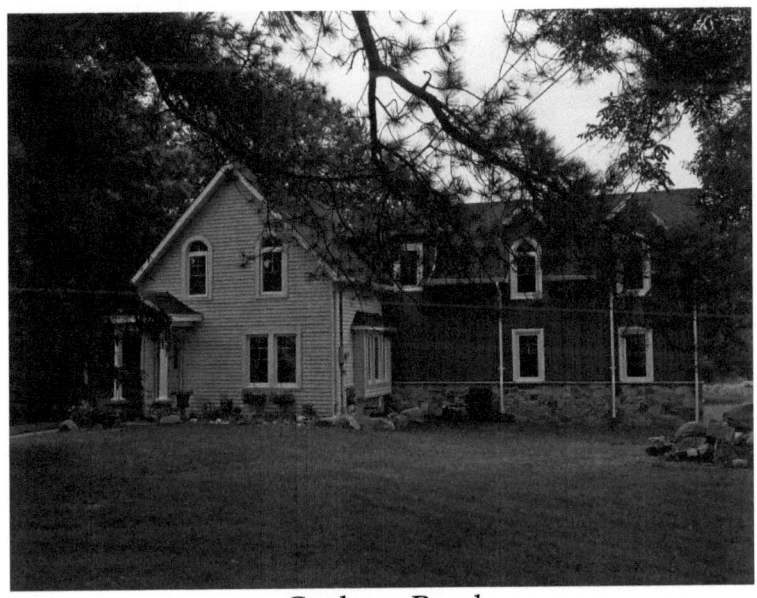

Canboro Road

Fonthill

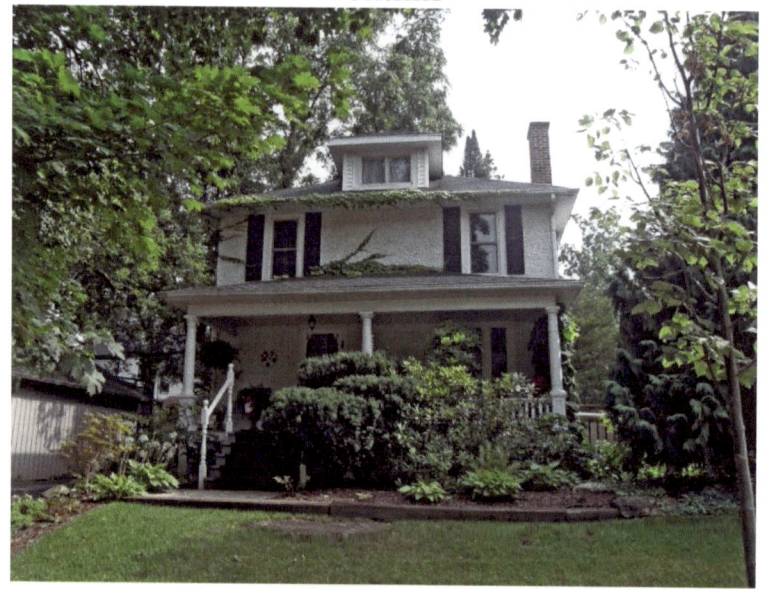

Elm Avenue - dormer

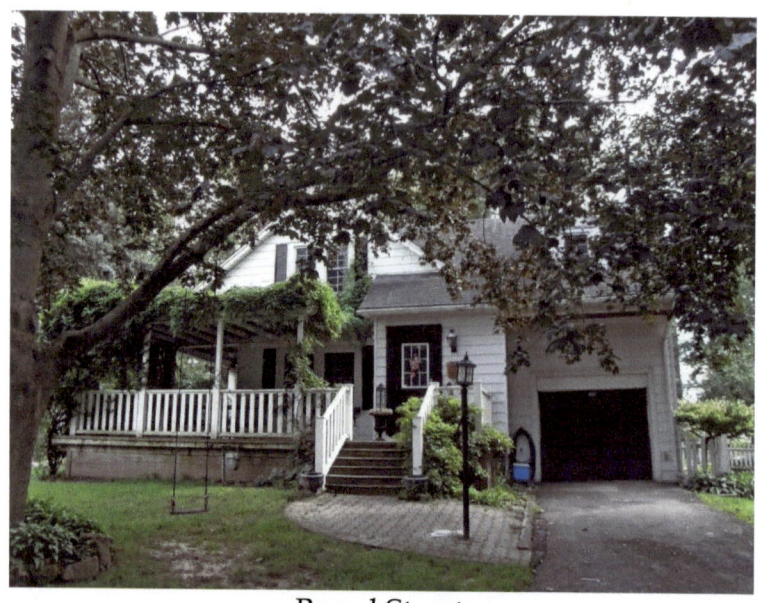

Broad Street

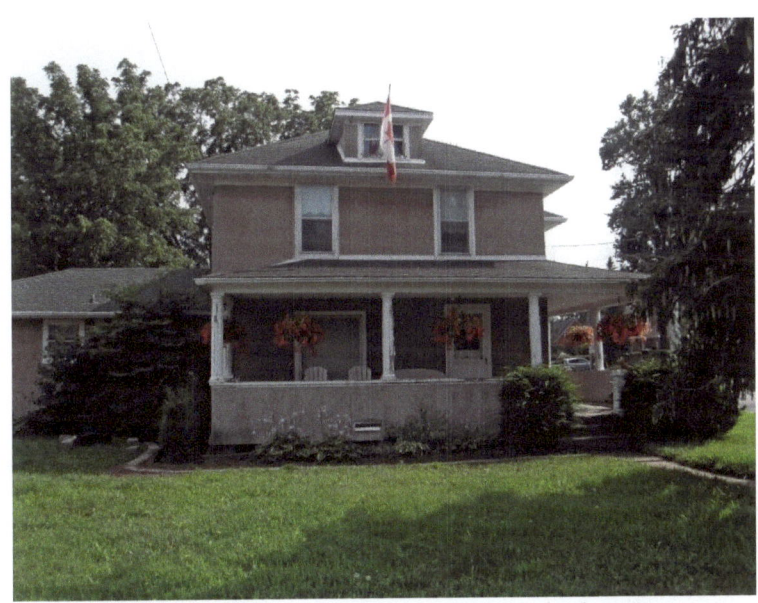

Canboro Road – hipped roof with dormer

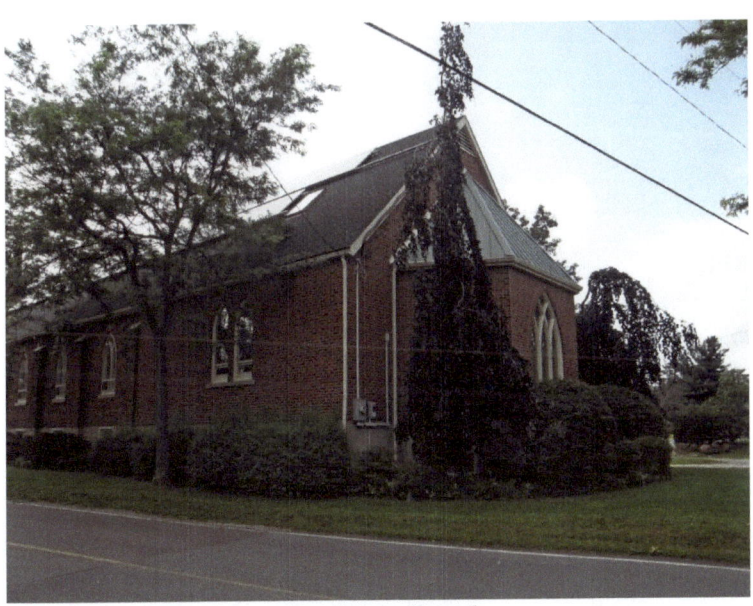

Canboro Road

Fonthill

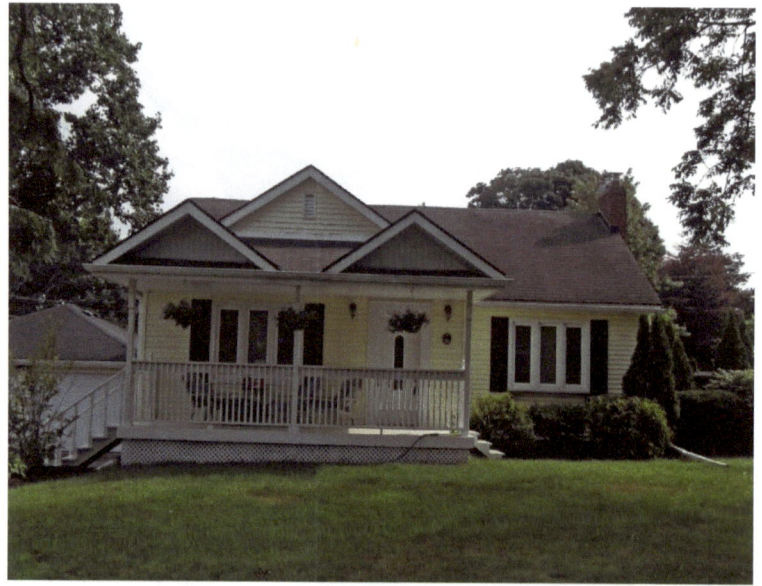

68 Canboro Road - pediments

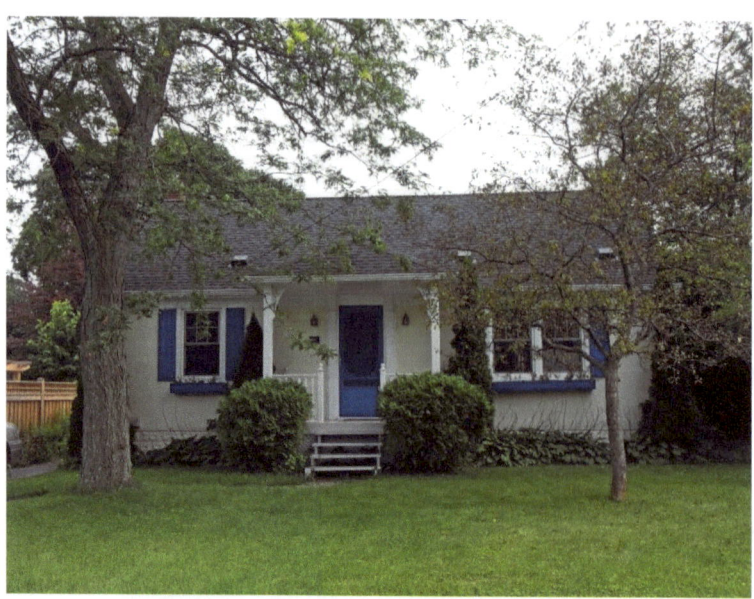

Canboro Road – Regency Cottage

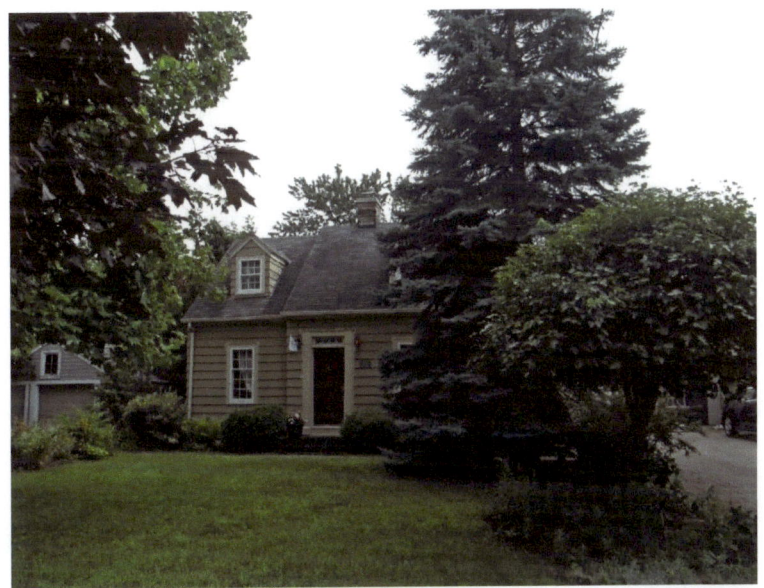
76 Canboro Road

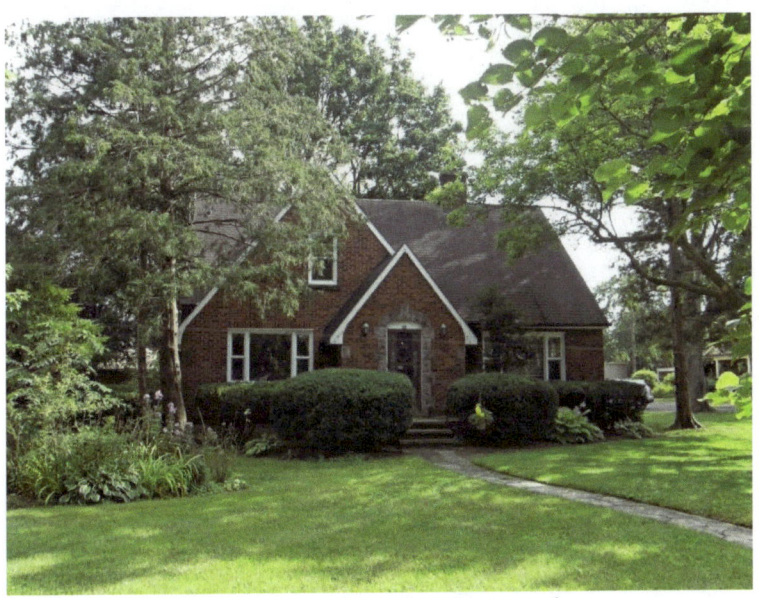
82 Canboro Road - Vernacular

Fonthill

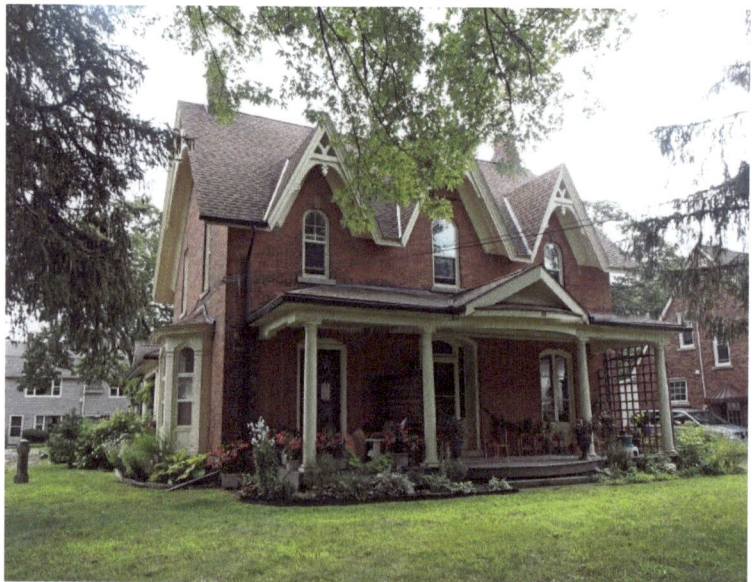

90 Canboro Road – The Wilson-Hansler-Stirtzinger House was built by John Wilson in 1876 of triple brick in the Gothic style. The walls are two feet thick and the floors are made of a mixture of cherry and maple woods. There is verge board trim on the gables, and a pediment above the door with sidelights and transom windows. The house passed onto the family of Dr. John Hansler, and then to his nephew John Loyal Stirtzinger in 1926. The house still remains on the property owned by descendants of Stirtzinger. Outside the house, the original Hansler carriage step and one of the hitching posts still stands.

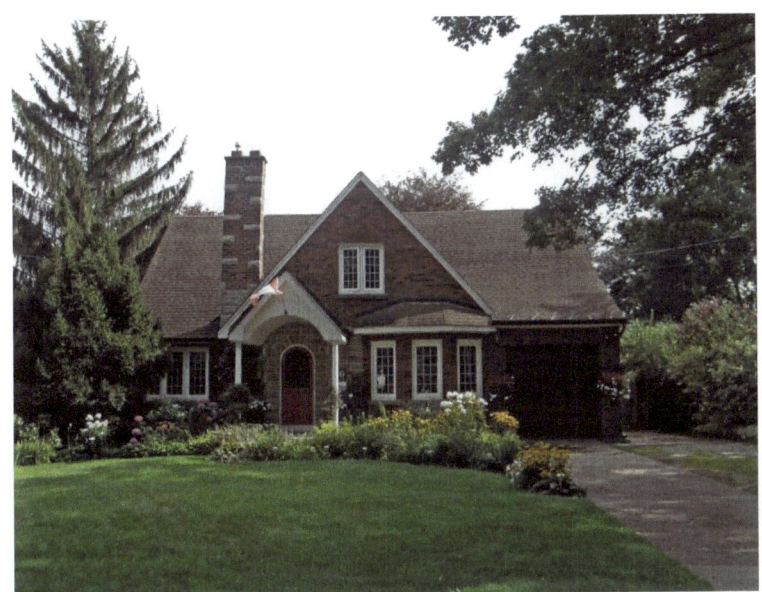

80 Canboro Road – bay window

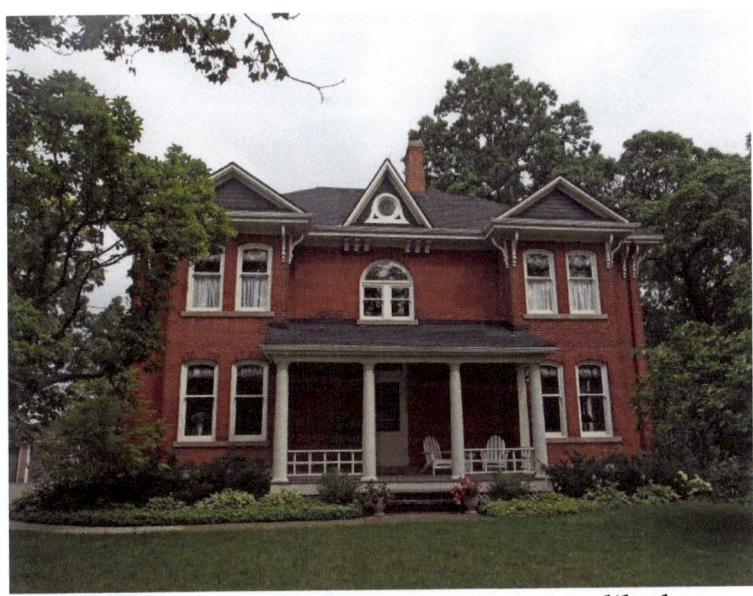

Chestnut Street – Italianate, two-storey tower-like bays each topped with a pediment, cornice brackets

Fonthill

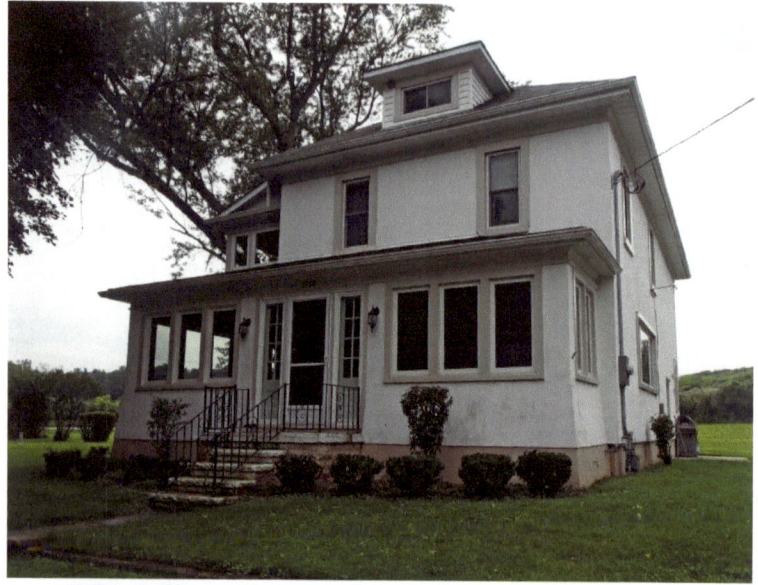

1796 Pelham Street – hipped roof with dormer

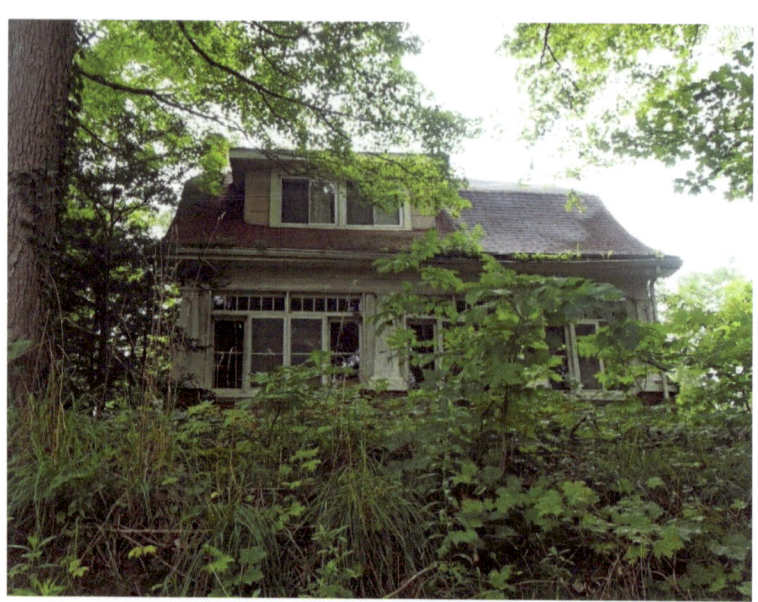

Pelham Street – shed dormer

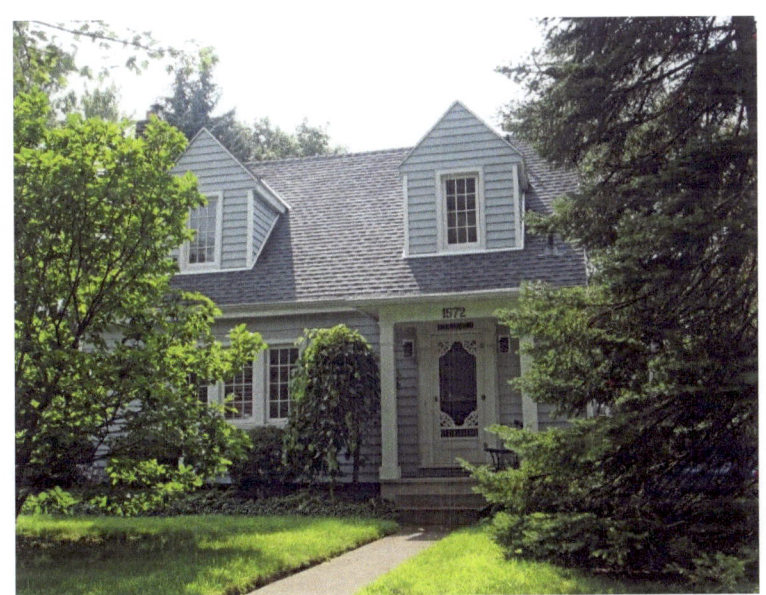
1572 Pelham Street - dormers

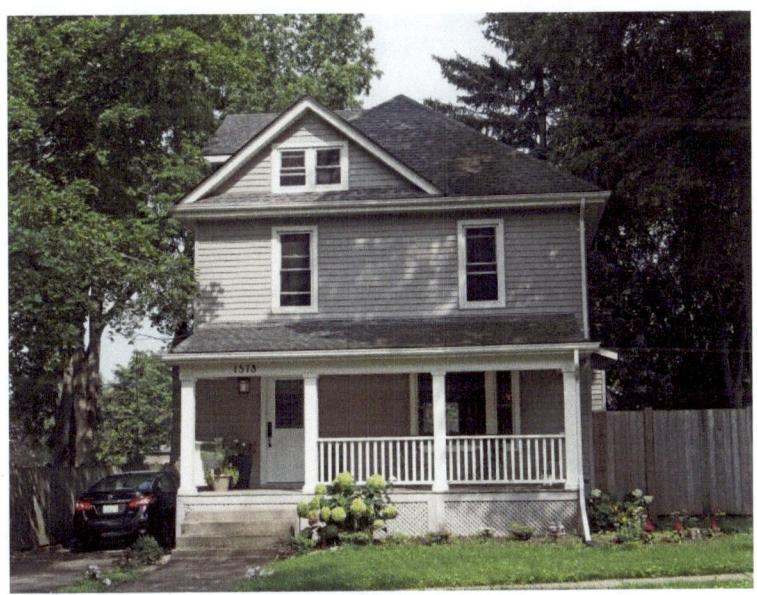
1573 Pelham Street

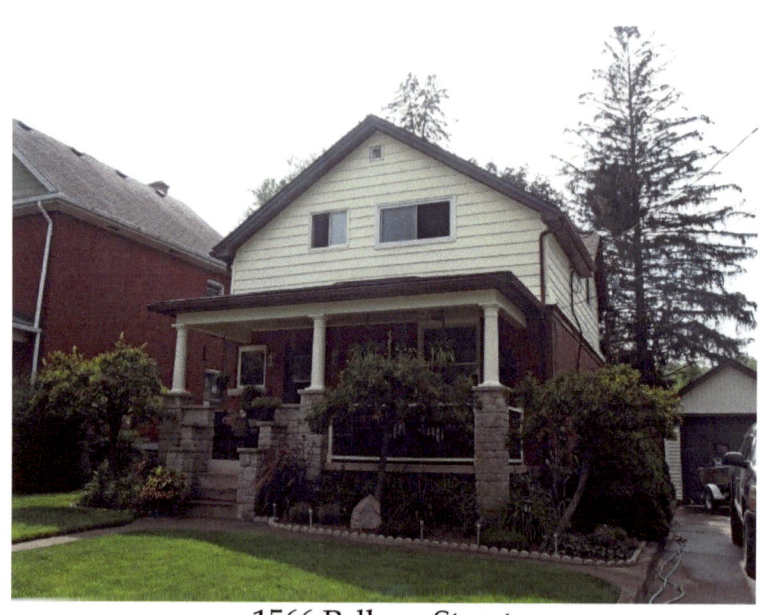

1566 Pelham Street

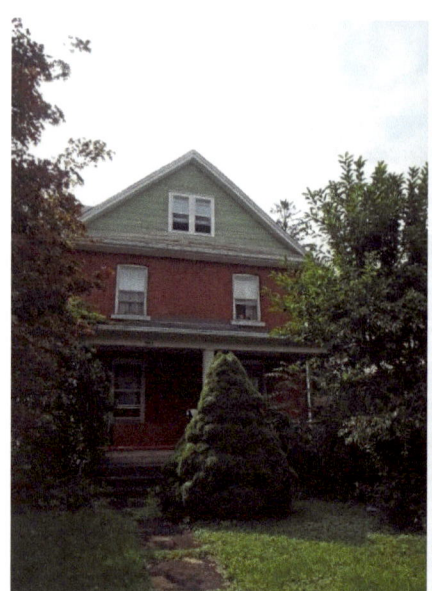

1564 Pelham Street
Edwardian

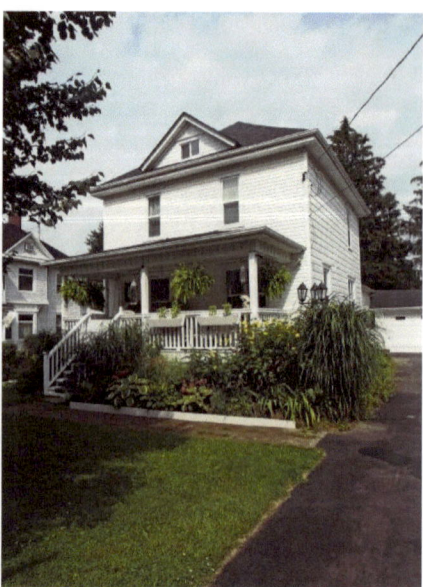

1565 Pelham Street
hipped roof

Fonthill

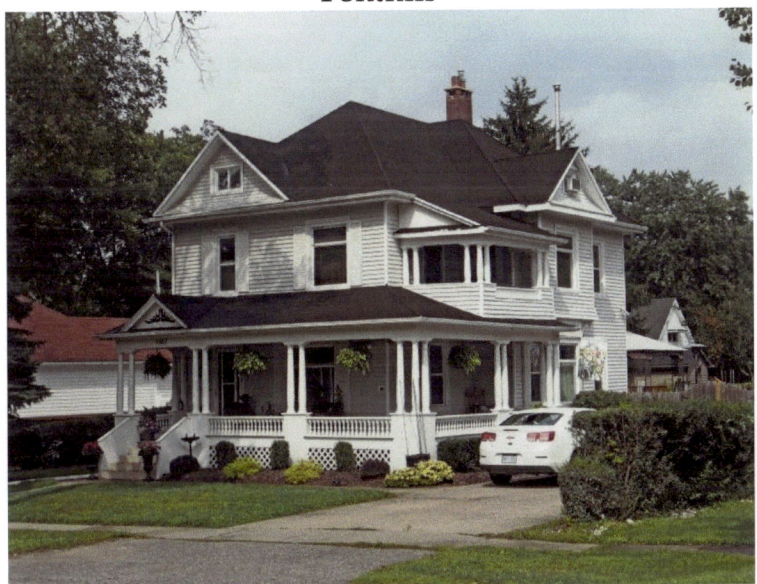

1567 Pelham Street

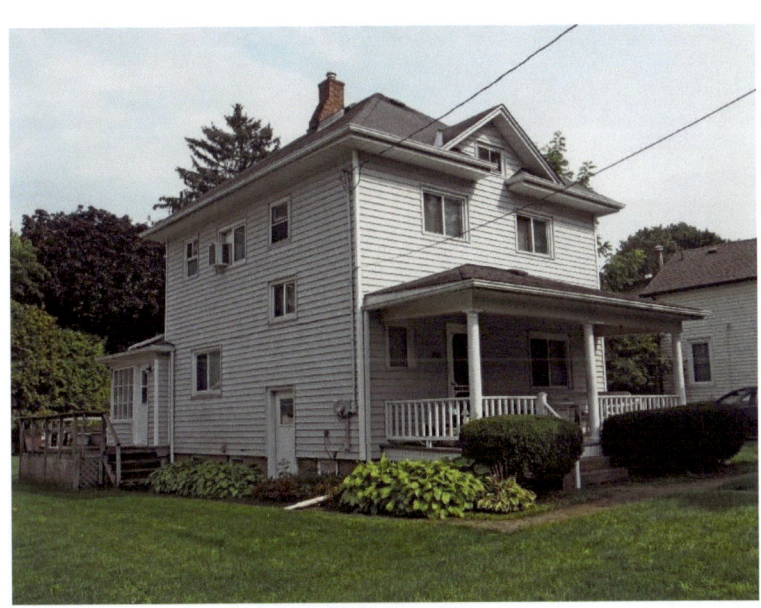

1561 Pelham Street

Fonthill

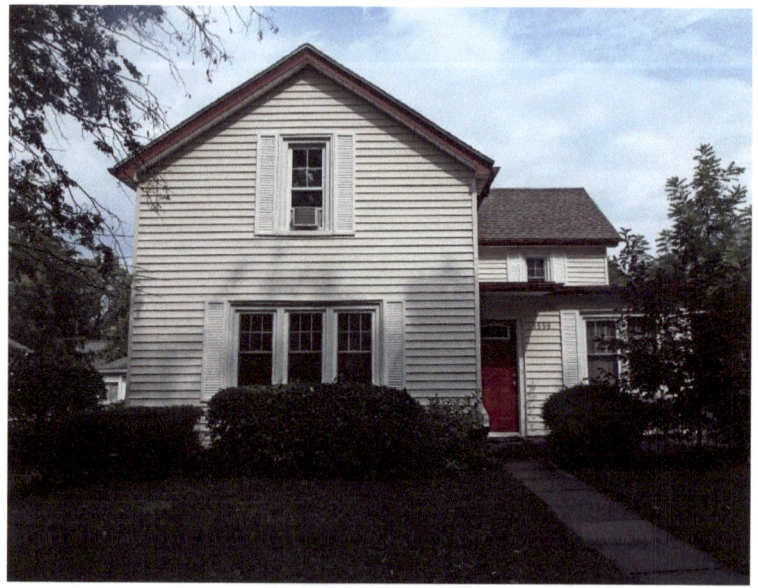

1559 Pelham Street

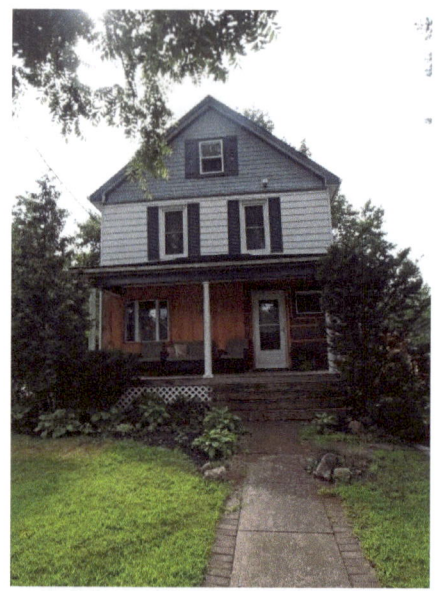

Pelham Street - Edwardian

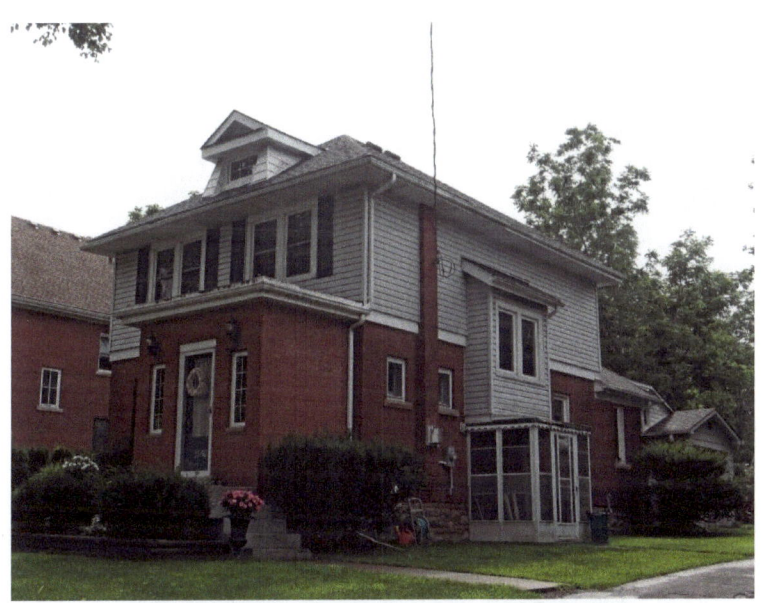

1556 Pelham Street – dormer in attic

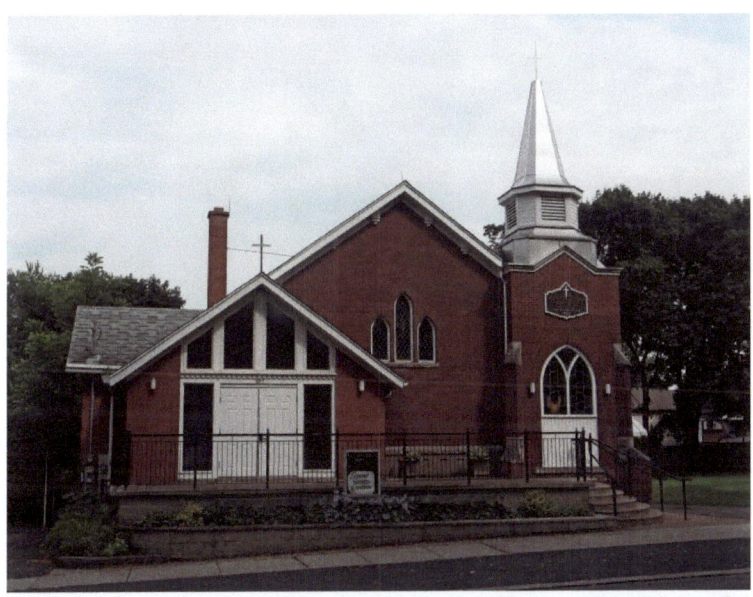

1557 Pelham Street – Holy Trinity Anglican Church – 1958 – lancet windows, tower

Fonthill

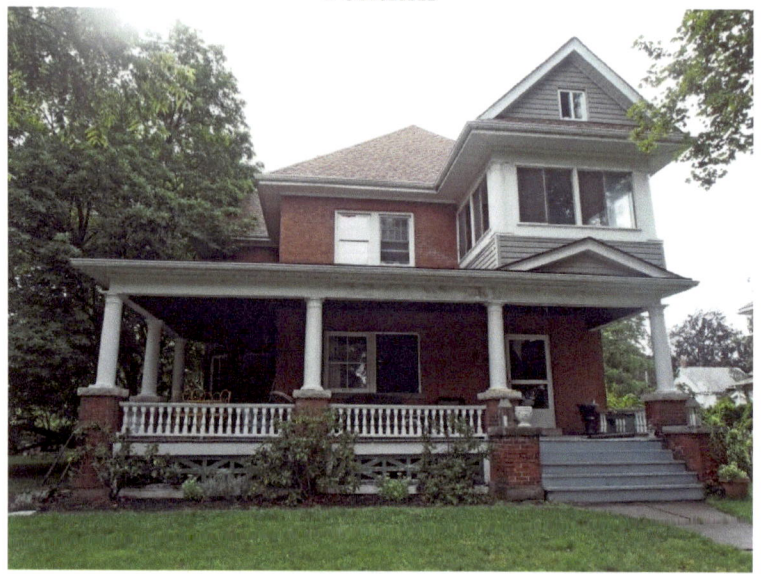

Pelham Street

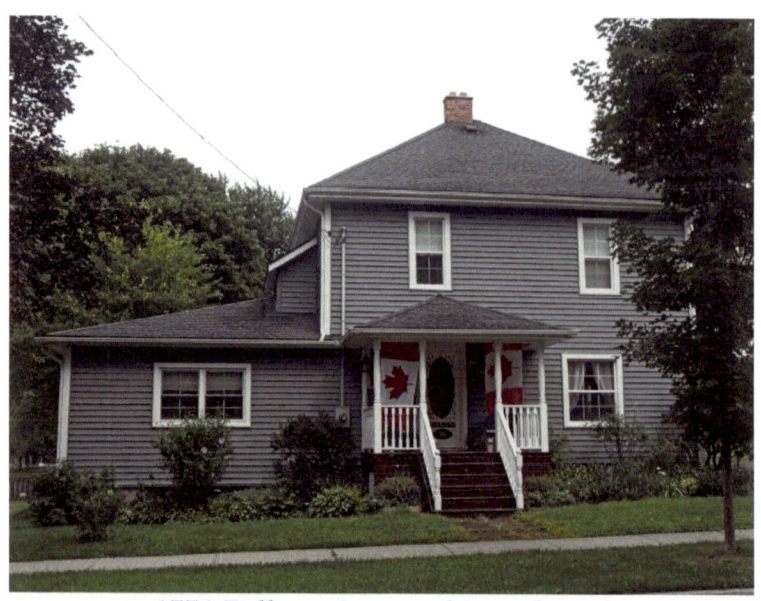

1551 Pelham Street – hipped roof

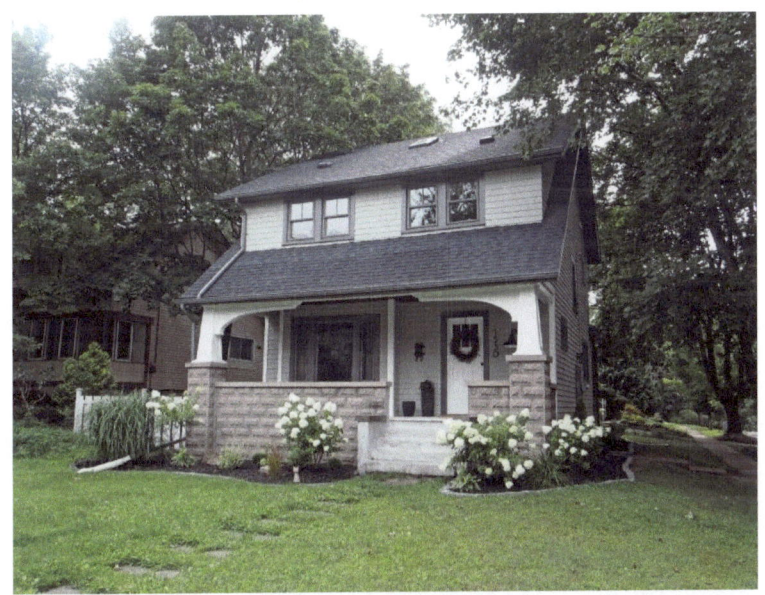

1550 Pelham Street

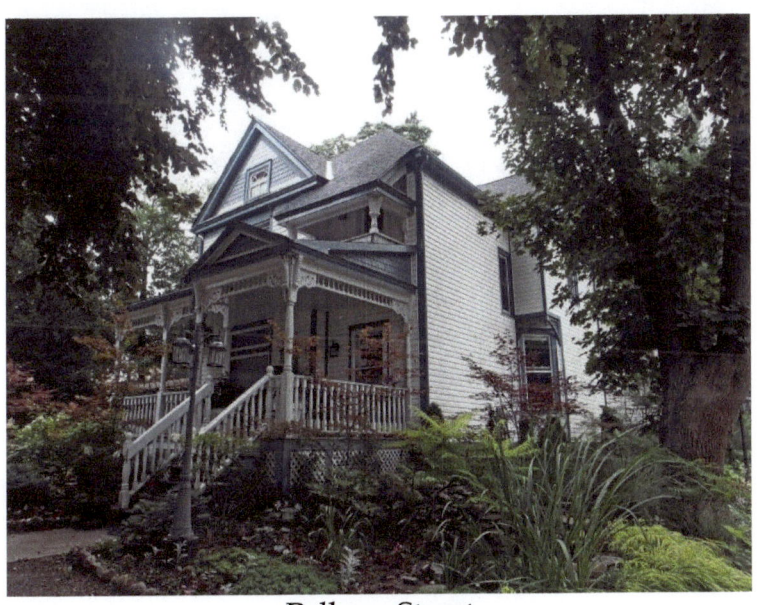

Pelham Street

1544 Pelham Street – The Fred Kinsman House was built in 1894 in the Queen Anne Revival style. The houses in this area of Pelham Street were built in the early 1900s on land once farmed by Henry Giles. He bought twenty-five acres here in 1843 and built his homestead near to the ravine. Henry died in 1871, and sometime later his house burned down.

There are three houses on this part of Pelham Street associated with the Kinsman family who ran the Kinsman's store on the south-east corner of Hwy 20. Earnest Kinsman, the third generation proprietor of the store, lived at 1550. Next door (1548) was the home of Jesse McCombs owner of McCombs Nursery. Number 1544 was built for Fred Kinsman, the second generation owner of Kinsman's and the village postmaster.

The house at 1522 was built in the mid-nineteenth century, and occupied by Danson Kinsman, who came to Fonthill from Nova Scotia and started the Kinsman's store in 1862. His son, Fred, was born in this house. From 1895-1923 it was the Baptist Church parsonage, and after that the home of Harry Brown a veterinarian and the local Sheriff.

Danson Kinsman was born in the township of Cornwallis, King's County, Nova Scotia, on April 23, 1813. His parents were Benjamin Avery and Mary (English) Kinsman, both natives of Nova Scotia. Benjamin was a descendant of the English family of Kinsmans who crossed the Atlantic in the "Mayflower." Danson received his education in Nova Scotia, and was married there on September 19, 1839, to Elizabeth, a daughter of John and Abigail (Foster) Douglas. In 1850, Mr. Kinsman moved with his wife and four children to Ontario and settled at Fonthill, where he engaged in the mercantile business. In 1864 he was appointed postmaster at Fonthill, a position which he held for many years. He had six children, John Douglas, who worked with a large insurance company in New York City; Avery, who was a resident of Rochester, New York; James who was a traveler for a hardware manufacturing company in Philadelphia; Anson traveled for a Detroit dry goods house; Hattie, the only daughter, is the wife of Torrence Lamb, of Brockport, New York; and Fred, the youngest son took over running the mercantile business in Fonthill in 1884.

Fred Kinsman, a son of Danson, was born on October 14, 1862. He received his education at the Fonthill Public School and the Welland High School. In addition to the business experience he had acquired at his father's store, he worked with a Toronto dry goods house before taking over from his father at Fonthill in February 1884. He carried out a very extensive trade, always keeping large stocks of dry goods, groceries, boots and shoes, hardware, etc.

Fonthill

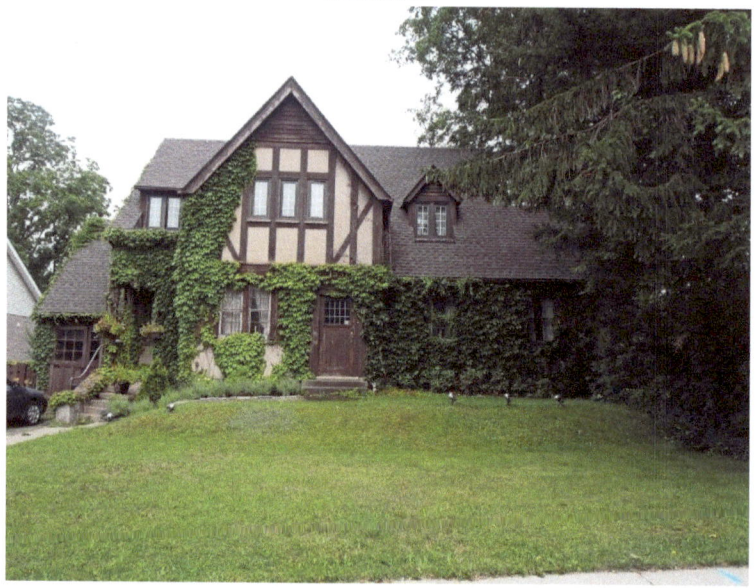

Pelham Street - Tudor

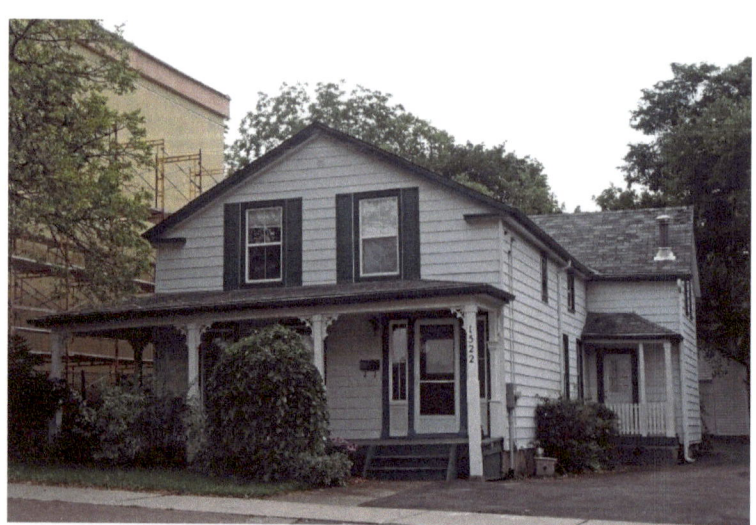

1552 Pelham Street – cornice return, bric-a-brac on veranda

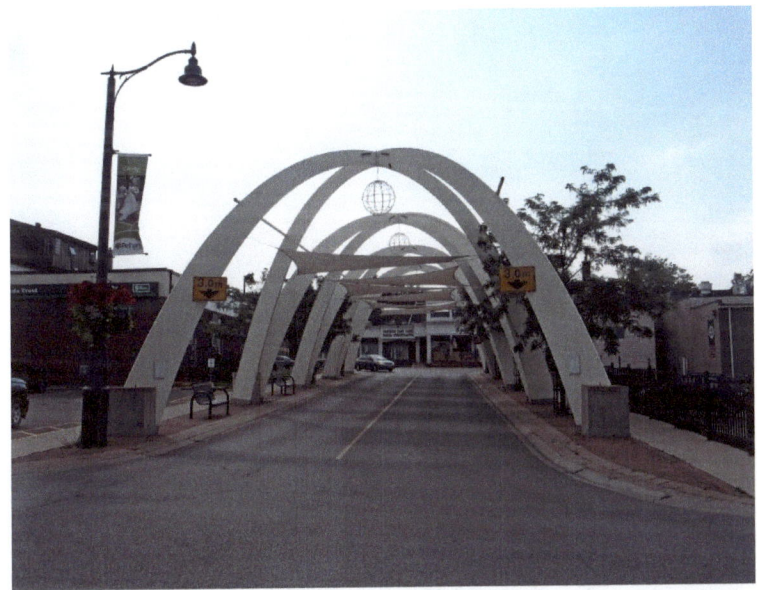

Pelham Arches – built 2012 – were designed to be a temporary installation for Pelham Summerfest to create a link between Pelham Street, the Town Square, and Peach Park festivities. The Arches were so well received by the community it was decided to have the structure remain for future events.

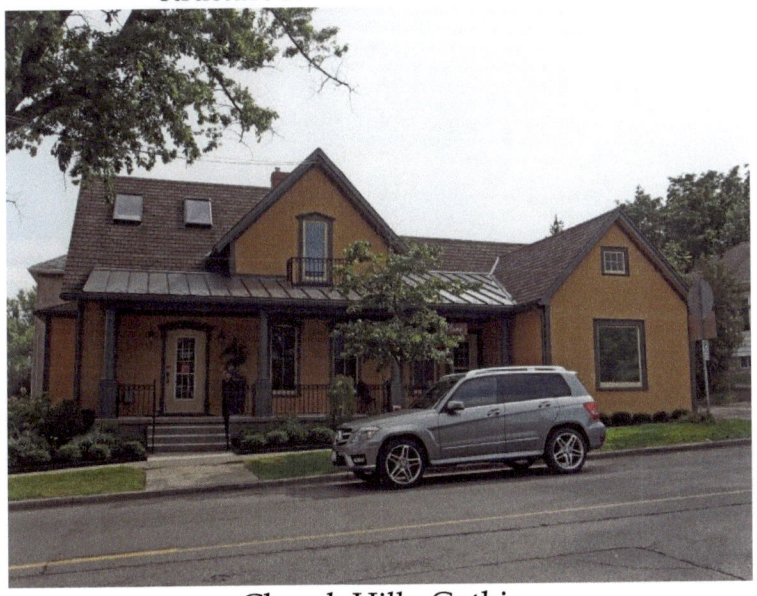

Church Hill - Gothic

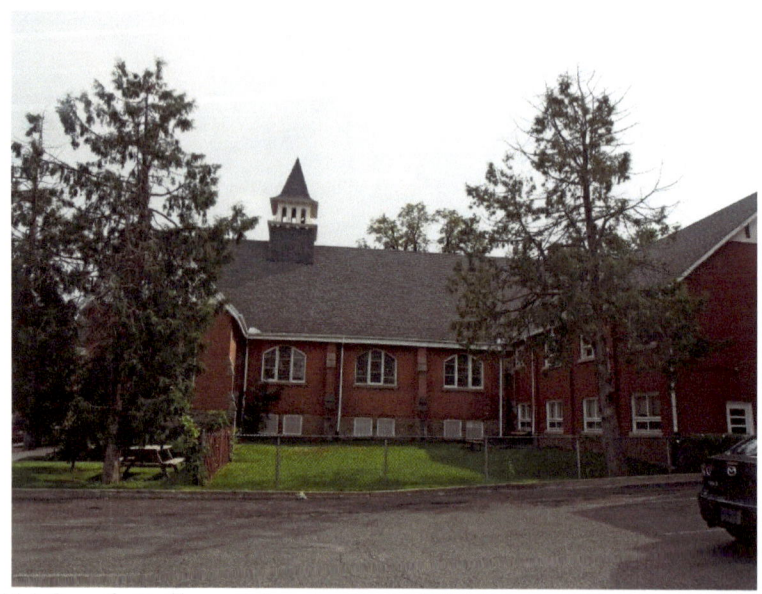

1414 South Pelham Street - Fonthill Baptist Church – 1909 – cupola on roof

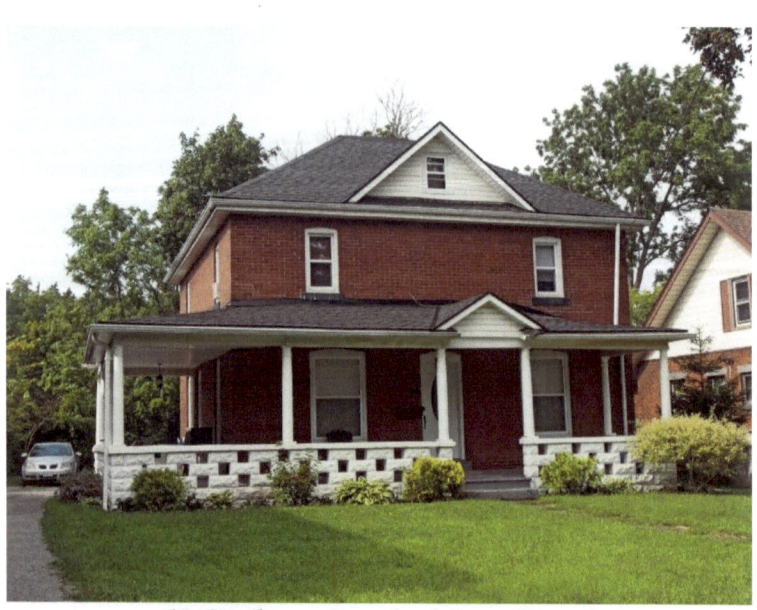

61 Canboro Road – hipped roof

Fonthill

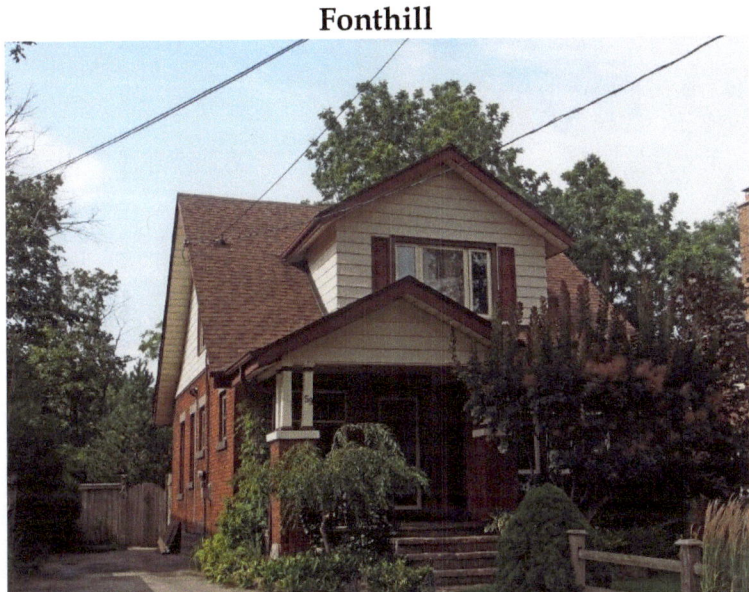

59 Canboro Road

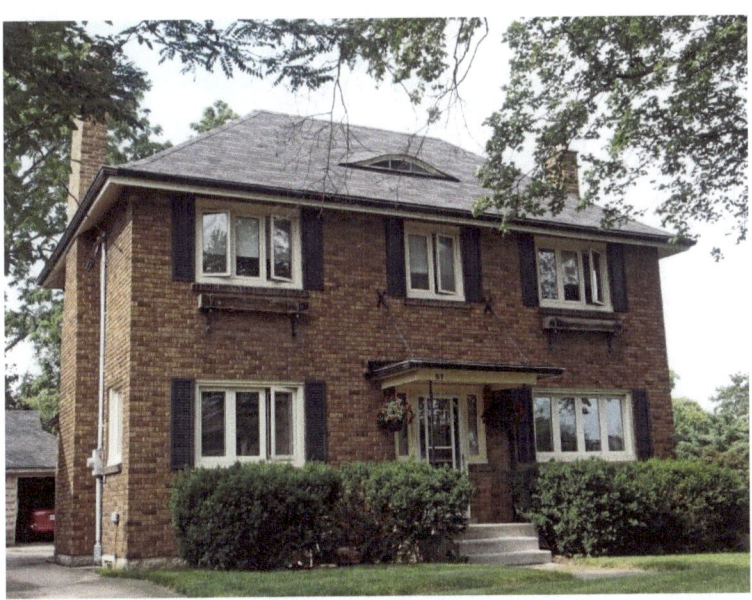

57 Canboro Road – hipped roof with eyebrow window, balanced façade

Fonthill

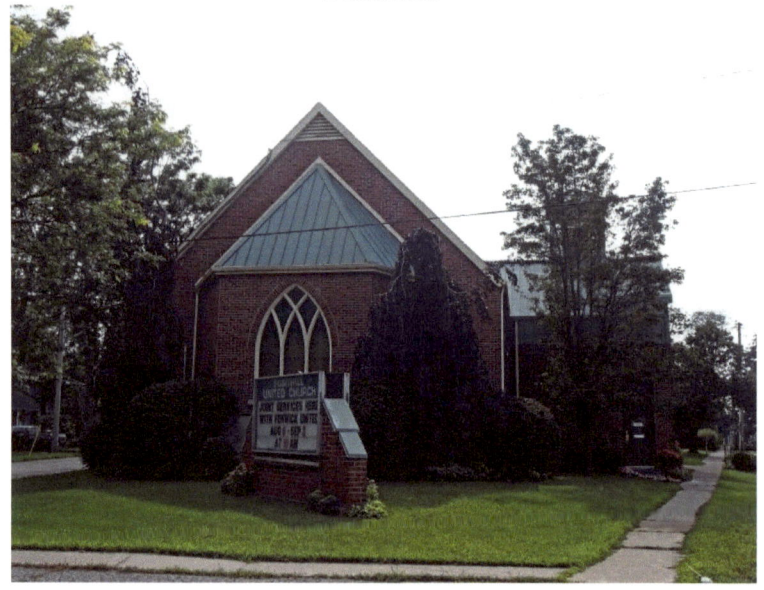

42 Church Hill - Fonthill United Church

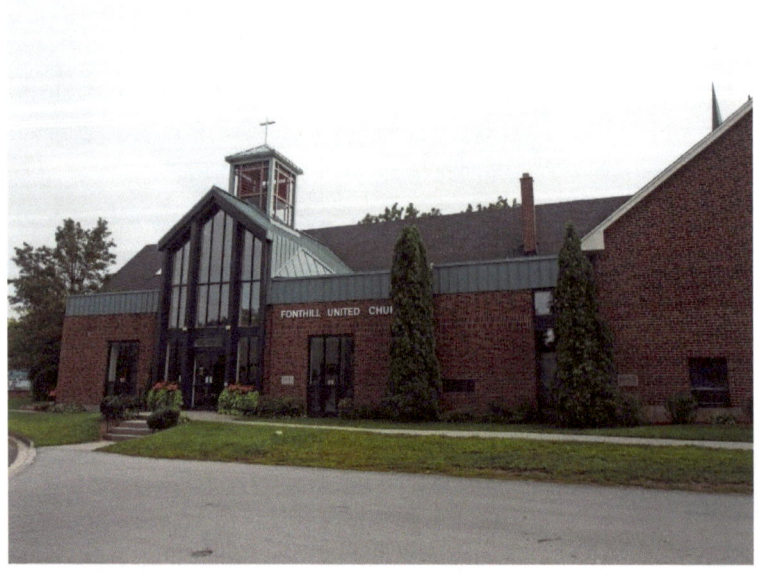

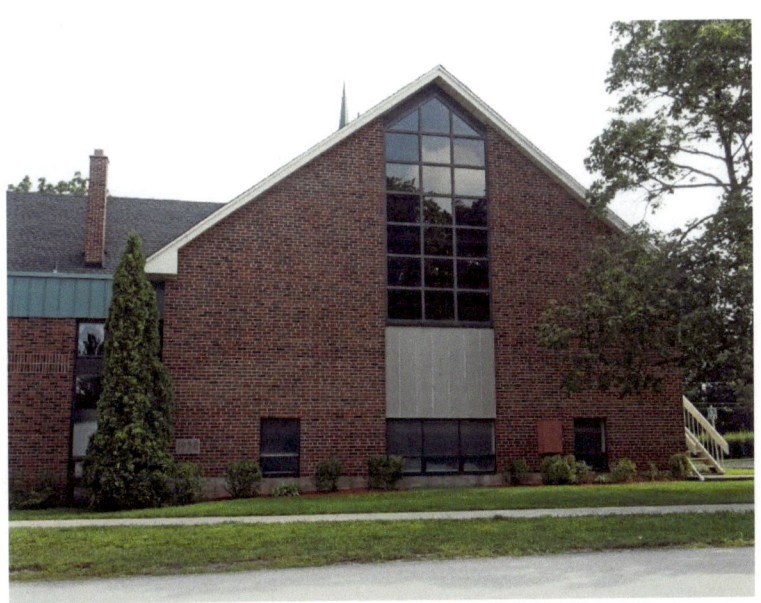
42 Church Hill - Fonthill United Church

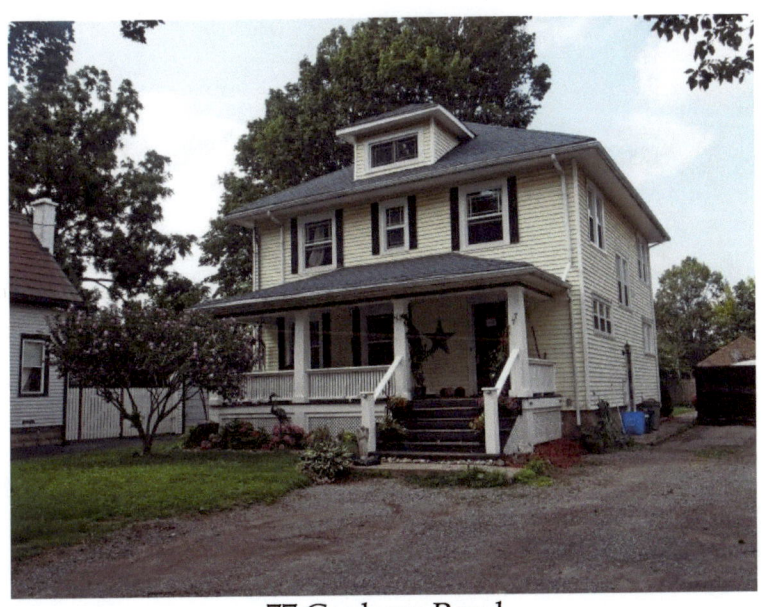
77 Canboro Road

Fonthill

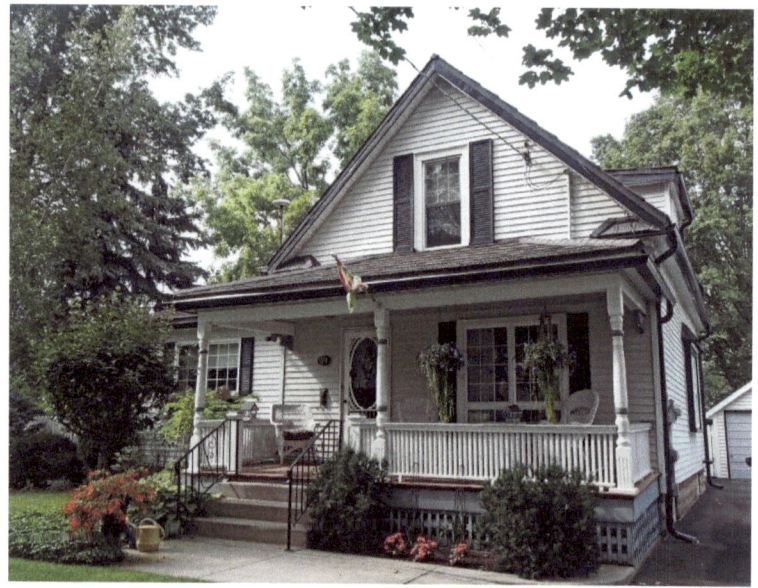

79 Canboro Road

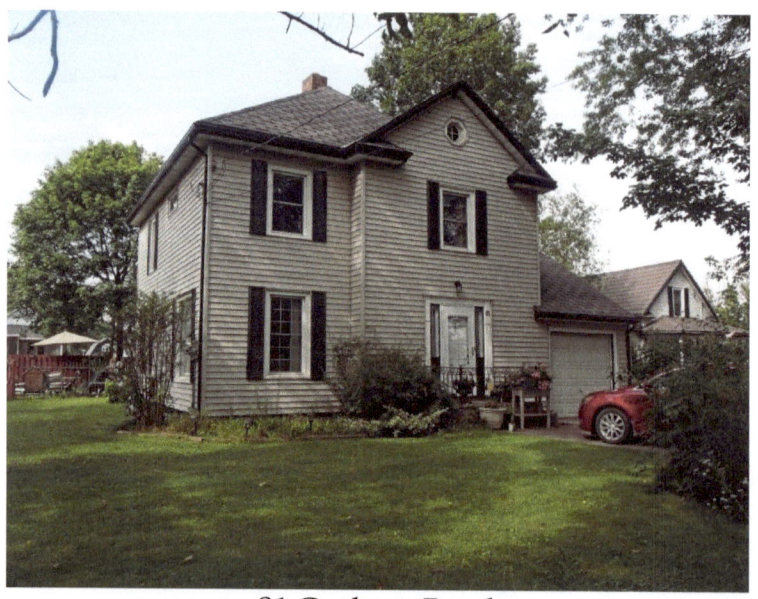

81 Canboro Road

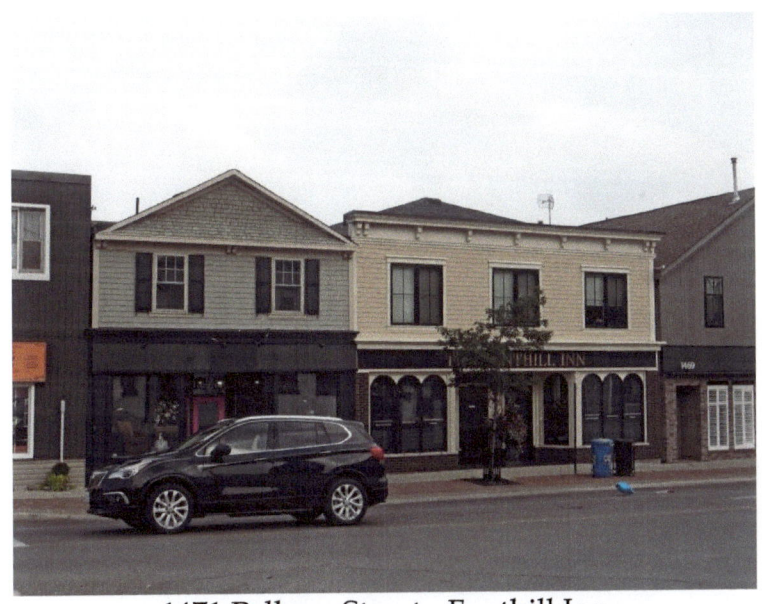

1471 Pelham Street - Fonthill Inn

Fonthill was known in earlier days as Osborne's Corners and Temperanceville, and grew up around an inn along busy Canboro Road. The two-story frame building, much altered, is located near the intersection of Regional Road 20 and Pelham Street. The Fonthill Inn is one of the oldest buildings in the Town of Pelham. A tavern was built on this site to service traffic on the "Great West Road" (the Canboro Road) probably before 1830. The owner was Jacob Osborne, and the settlement that grew up round it was first called Osborne's Corners. After the name Fonthill was adopted for the village, the tavern became the Fonthill Hotel, for many years a "temperance hotel". It narrowly escaped the fire of 1888, and in the twentieth century has been used for a variety of stores and businesses.

Pelham

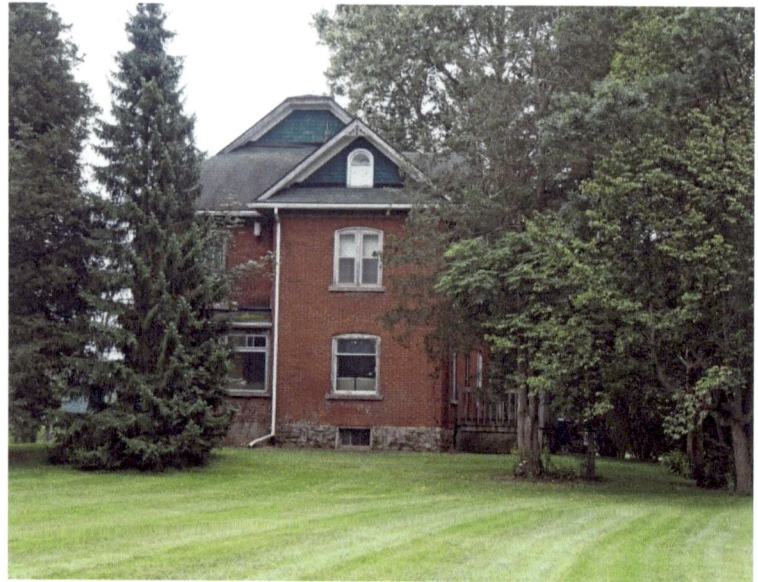

778 Tice Road

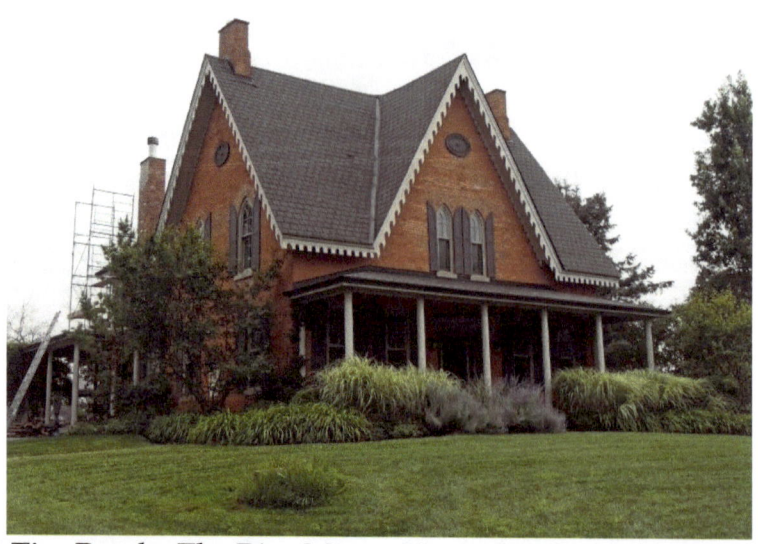

711 Tice Road – The Rice Moore House has been designated a heritage site for its architectural value. There is barge board trim around roofline, and steeply pitched gables.

Balfour Street was named after Walter and Jean Balfour who lived here in the 1920s; it was also known as the Pelham Stone Road.

In the Village of North Pelham on Balfour Street, there are some Victorian Villas dating back to the 19th Century, one of which is known as the Horton House.

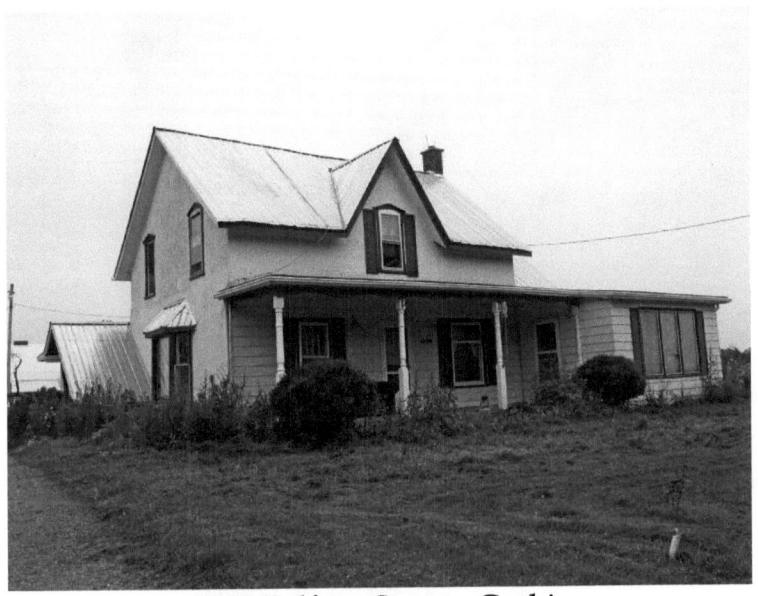

1560 Balfour Street - Gothic

Pelham

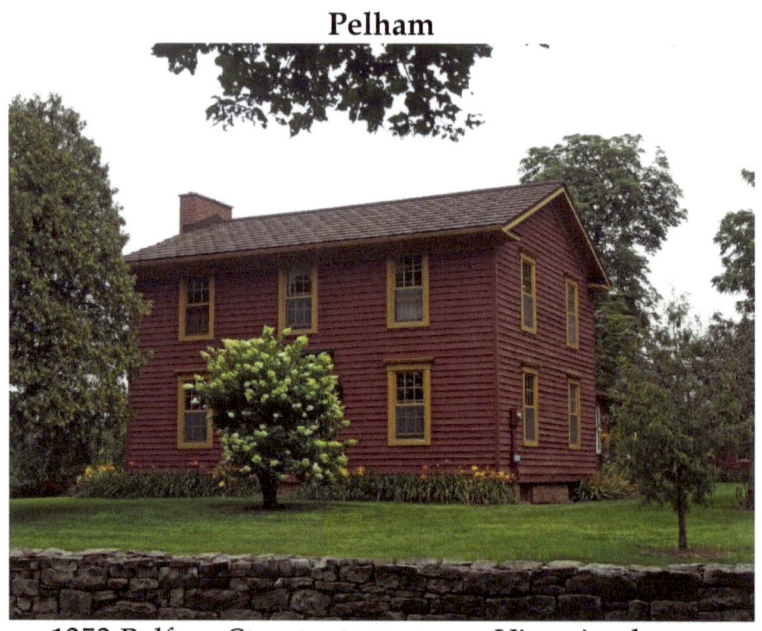

1353 Balfour Street – two-storey Victorian house

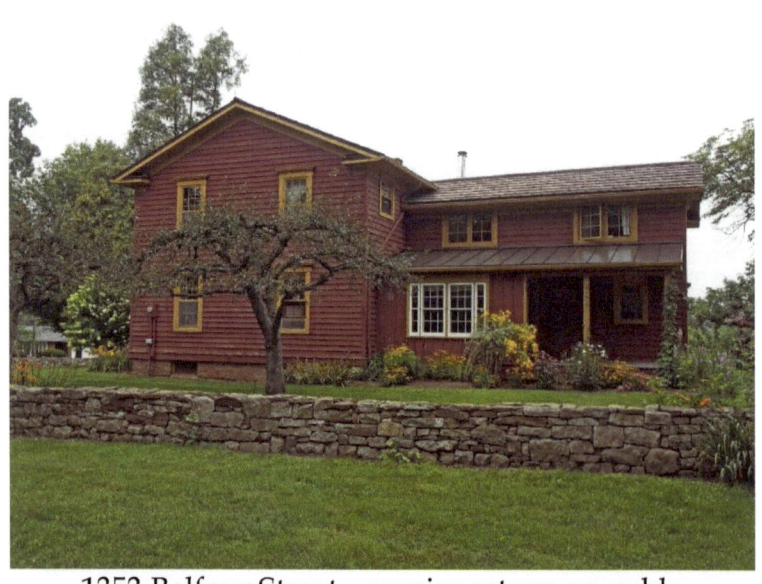

1353 Balfour Street - cornice return on gable

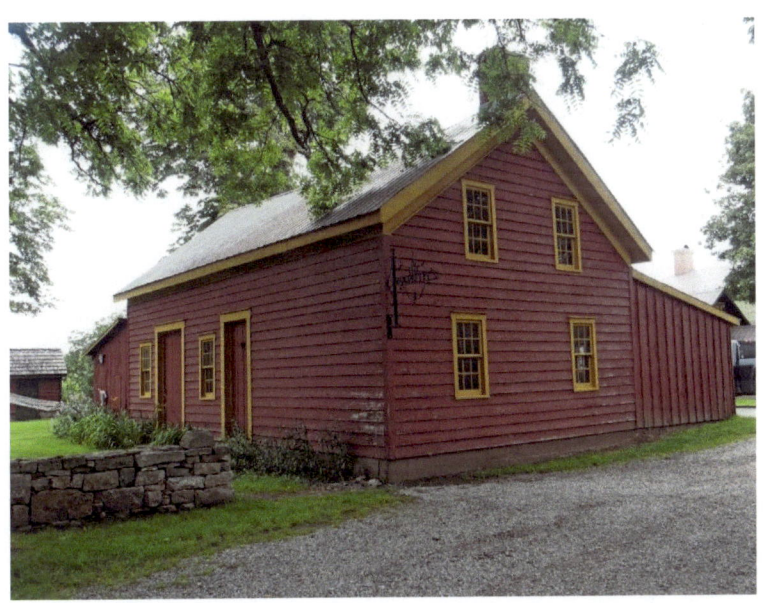

1353 Balfour Street

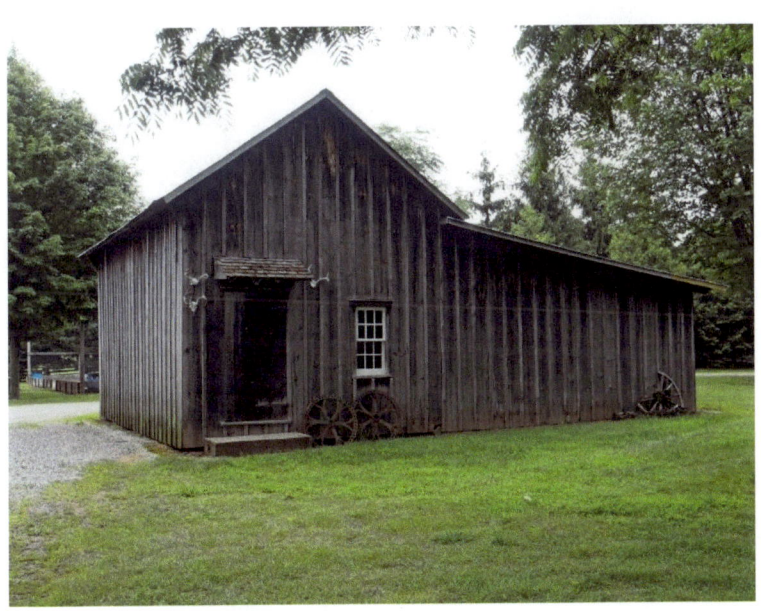

Pelham

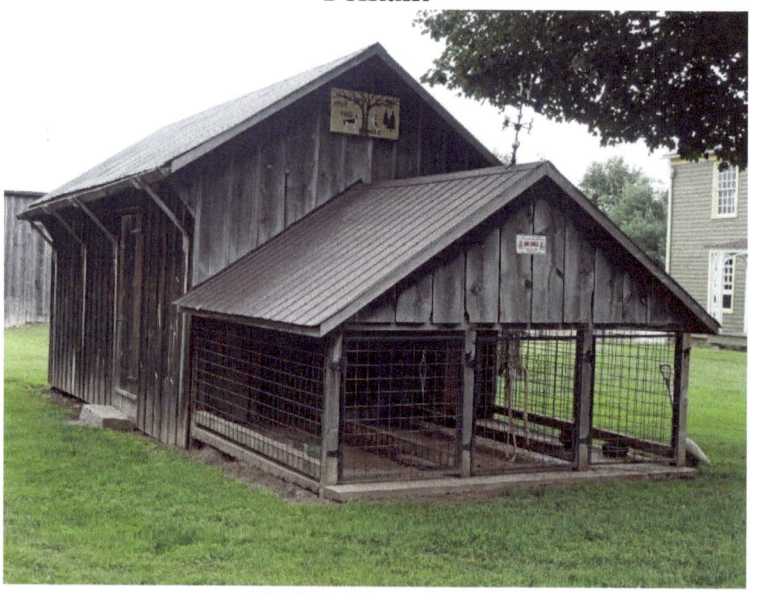

1353 Balfour Street

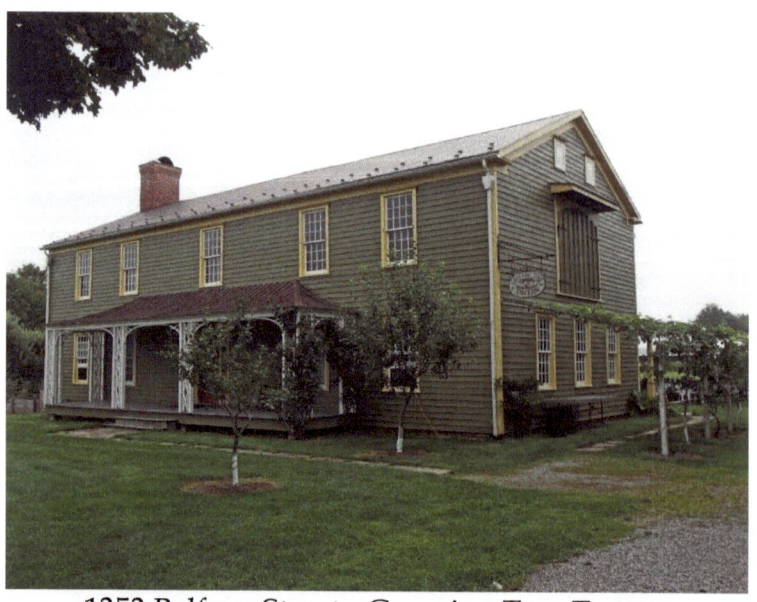

1353 Balfour Street - Greening Tree Tavern

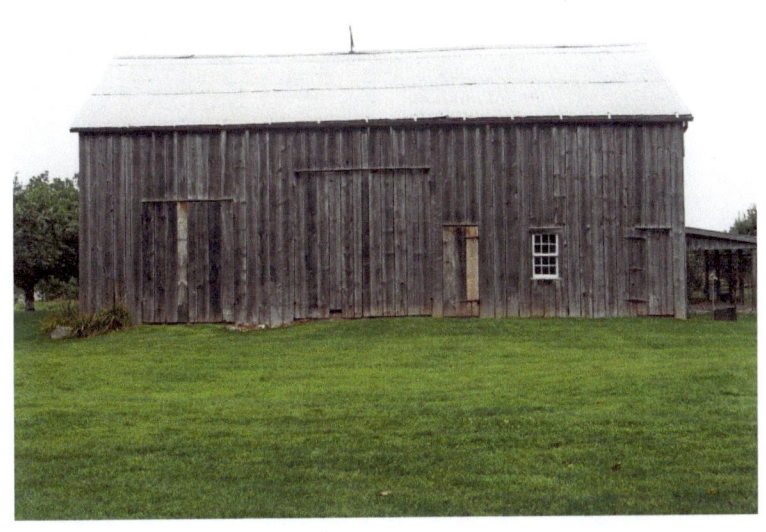

1353 Balfour Street

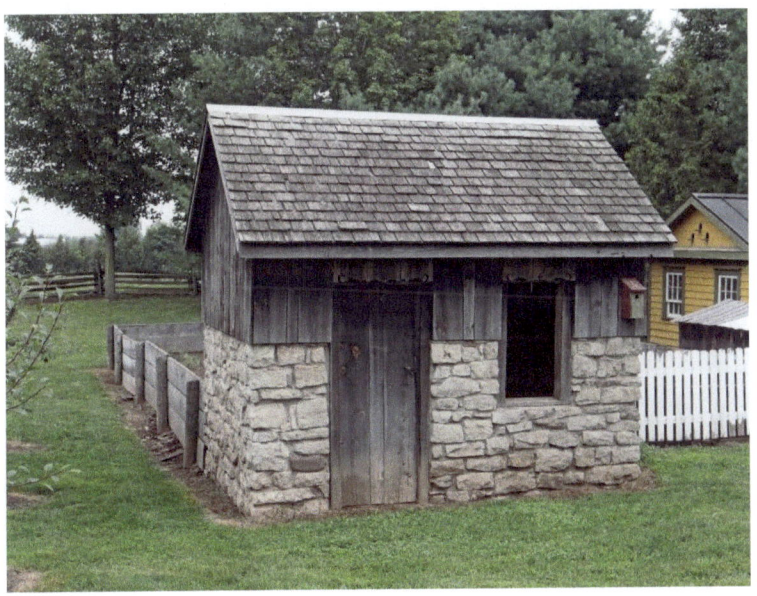

Pelham

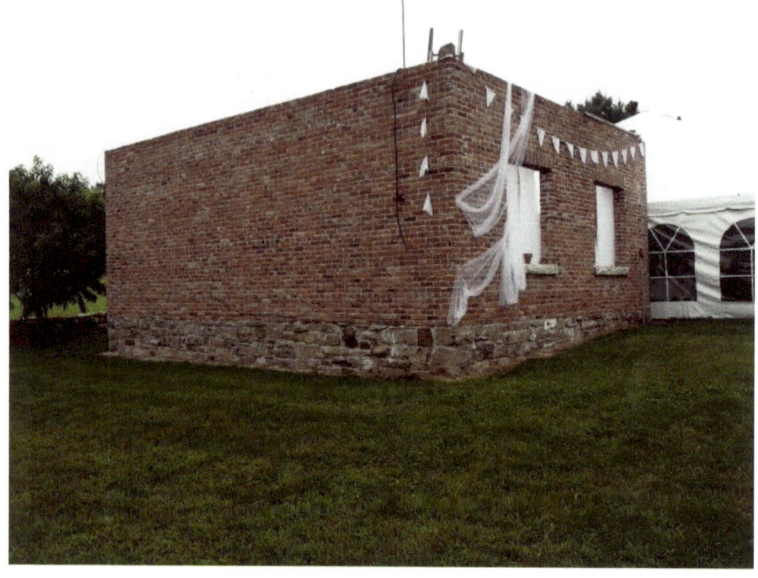

1353 Balfour Street

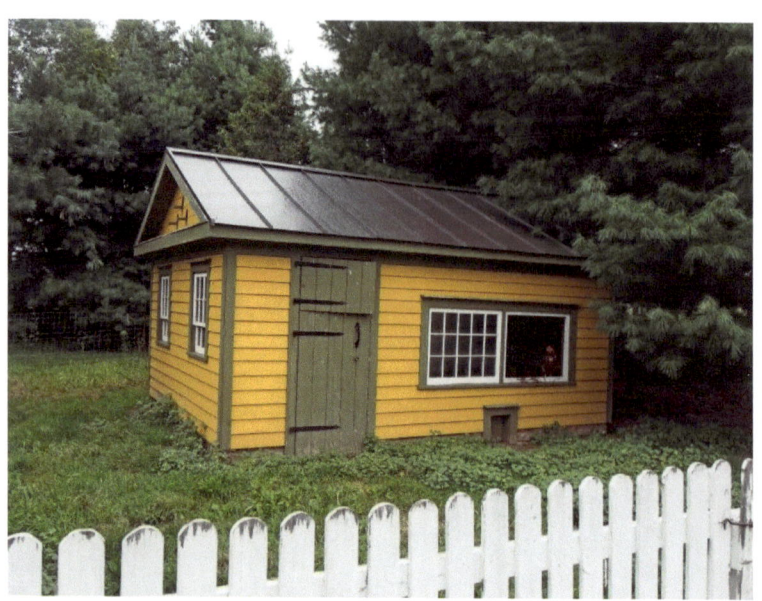

1353 Balfour Street

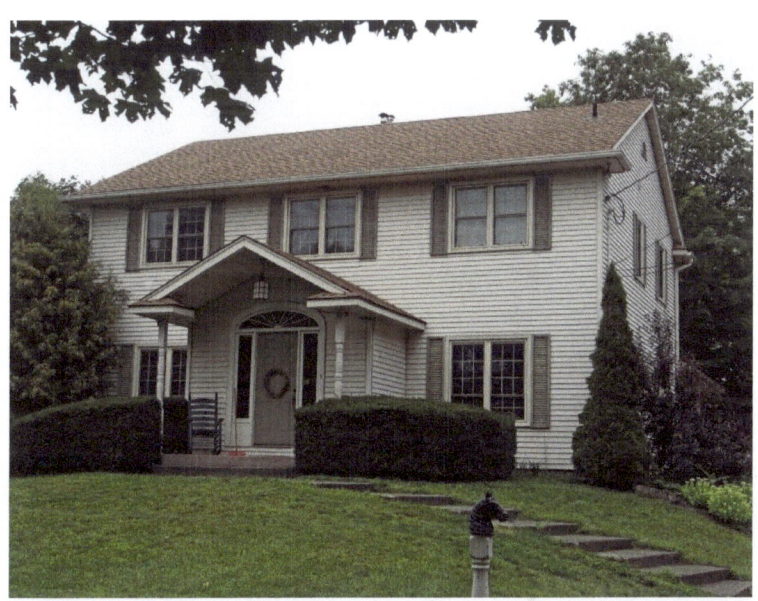

1341 Balfour Street –sidelights and transom windows around door

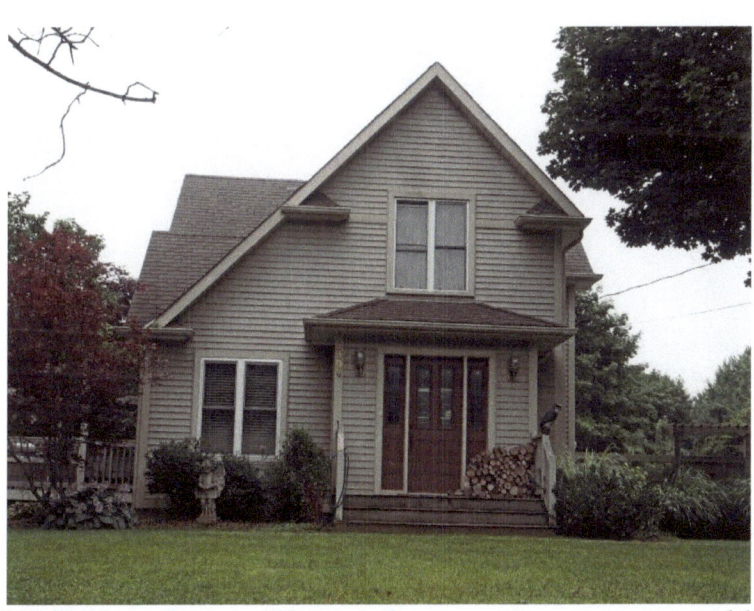

1304 Balfour Street – Vernacular - cornice return on gable, sidelights

Pelham

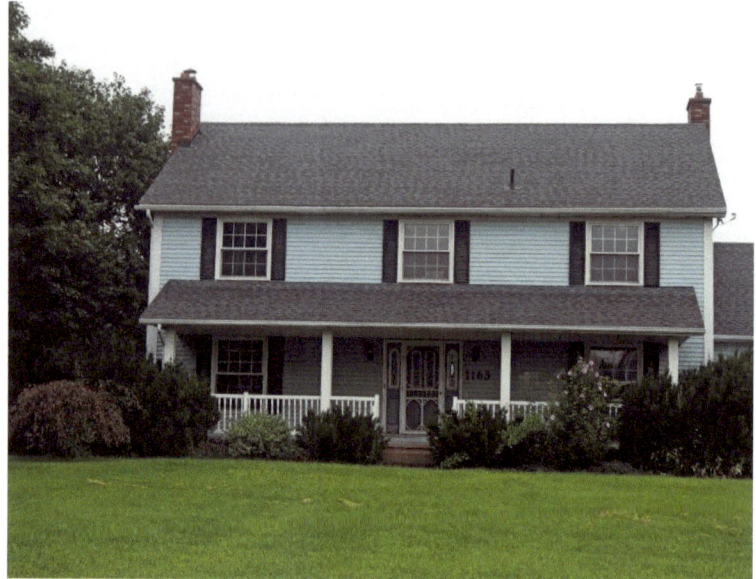

1163 Balfour Street – Georgian style – balanced façade

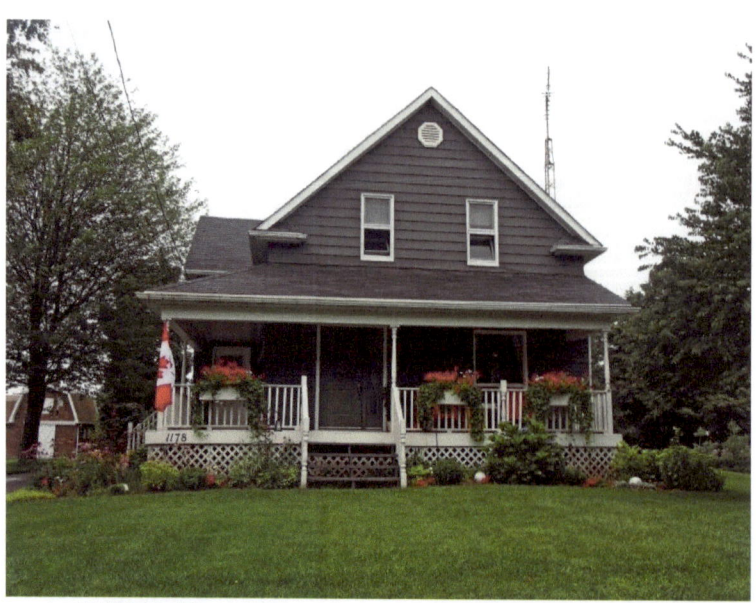

1178 Balfour Street – cornice return on gable

Architectural Terms

Bay Window: A window that projects out from a wall, in a semicircular, rectangular, or polygonal design. Used frequently in Gothic and Victorian designs. Example: Canboro Road, Page 11	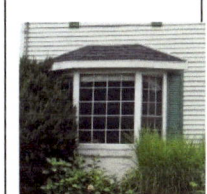
Brackets: a decorative or weight-bearing structural element which forms a right angle with one side against a wall and the other under a projecting surface such as an eave or roof. Example: 840 Canboro Road, Page 21	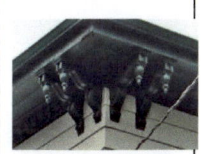
Cornice Return: decorative element on the end of a gable. Example: 759 Canboro Road, Page 12	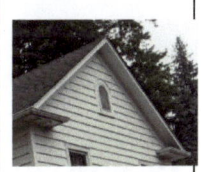
Cupola: A domed or curved roof rising from a building as a decorative element. Example: Canboro Road, Fenwick, Page 18	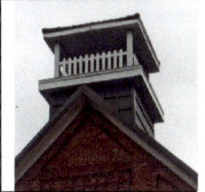
Dormer: (French for "sleep") a gable end window that pierces through the plane of a sloping roof surface to create usable space in the top floor or attic of a building by adding headroom. Example: 837 Canboro Road, Page 21	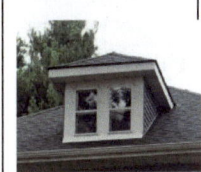

Gable: the triangular portion of a wall between the edges of a sloping roof. Example: 711 Tice Road, Page 51	
Hipped Roof: a roof where all sides slope downwards to the walls with no gables. Example: Canboro Road, Page 28	
Lancet Window: a tall, narrow window with a pointed arch at its top. Example: 1557 Pelham Street, Page 38	
Parapet: low wall around the edge of a roof. Example: Canboro Road, Page 15	
Pediment: a triangular section above the door or portico, usually supported by columns. The inside of the triangle is called the tympanum. Example: 68 Canboro Road, Page 29	
Quoin: masonry blocks at the corner of a wall, often a decorative feature, usually larger or of a different colour than the rest of the wall. Example: Canboro Road, Page 18	

Rose Window: a circular window with ornamental tracery radiating from the centre. Example: Canboro Road, Fenwick, Page 18	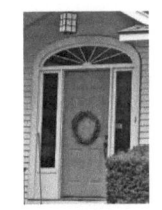
Sidelight: a vertical window that flanks a door, and is often used to emphasize the importance of a primary entrance. **Transom Window:** the light above the doorway, also called a fanlight. Example: 1341 Balfour Street, Page 58	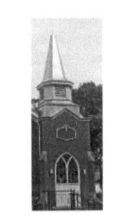
Tower: A circular, square, or octagonal vertical structure higher than the surrounding structure that is usually part of an existing building and is created either for extra defense or for a specific purpose such as a clock or a bell tower. Example: 1557 Pelham Street, Page 38	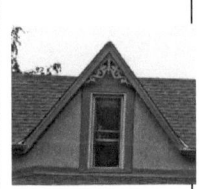
Verge board and Finial: also called bargeboards – hang from the projecting end of a roof and are often elaborately carved and ornamented. **Finial:** ornament added to the top of a gable, pinnacle, canopy or spire – a Gothic element. Example: Canboro Road, Page 25	

Building Styles

Edwardian, 1900-1930 – This style bridges the ornate and elaborate styles of the Victorian era and the simplified styles of the 20th century. Edwardian Classicism provided simple, balanced facades, simple rooflines, dormer windows, large front porches, and smooth brick surfaces. Voussoirs and keystones are used sparingly and are understated. Cornice brackets and braces are block-like and openings have flat arches or plain stone lintels. Example: 1564 Pelham Street, Page 35	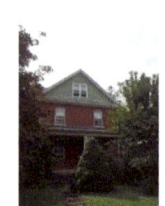
Georgian, before 1860 – This style began with the British King Georges in the 18th century. These buildings have balanced facades around a central door, medium-pitched gable roofs, and small paned windows. Example: Canboro Road, Page 20	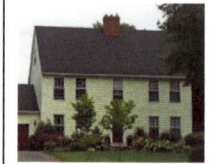
Gothic Revival, 1830-1890 – These decorative buildings have sharply-pitched gables with highly detailed verge boards, pointed-arch window openings, and dichromatic brickwork. It is a common style in Ontario. Example: 1560 Balfour Street, Page 52	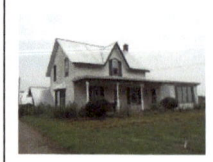

Italianate, 1850-1900 – A two story rectangular building with a mild hip roof, a projecting frontispiece, and generous eaves with ornate cornice brackets was the basis of the style; often there are large sash windows, quoins, ornate detailing on the windows, belvederes and wraparound verandahs. Italianate commercial buildings often have cast iron cresting and elegant window surrounds. Example: Chestnut Street, Page 32	
Regency Cottage, 1830-1860 – This style originated in England in 1815 and spread to Ontario later in the 19th century as British officers retired to Canada. It is a modest one-storey house with a low-pitched hip roof and has a symmetrical front façade. Example: Canboro Road, Page 29	
Tudor Revival – exposed timbers with stucco infill, multi-paned windows. Example: Pelham Street, Page 43	
Vernacular/Traditional Mode 1638 - 1950 Influenced but not defined by a particular style, vernacular buildings are made from easily available materials and exhibit local design characteristics. Example: 1304 Balfour Street, Page 58	

www.ingramcontent.com/pod-product-compliance
Lightning Source LLC
Chambersburg PA
CBHW040236220526

45473CB00001B/260

SHERIA ZA MIKOPO NA VYAMA VYA USHIRIKA TANZANIA.

Paulo Karlo Kalomo [Wakili]
Desemba, 2013

© **Paulo Karlo Kalomo [Wakili], 2013**
Haki zote zimehifadhiwa. Hairuhusiwi kukitoa kitabu au sehemu ya kitabu hiki kwa namna yoyote ile bila kufuata sheria na taratibu za haki miliki au kupata kibali cha maandishi kutoka kwa mwandishi chini ya Sheria ya Haki Miliki na Haki Shiriki Na. 7 ya mwaka 1999 [Marejeo ya mwaka 2002].

Kutohusika na Madai [Disclaimer Liability]: Wakati kila juhudi imefanyika ili kuondokana na makosa, usahaulifu au uachaji wa jambo lolote, mwandishi, mchapishaji na mpiga chapa hawatawajibika kwa madai yoyote au hasara kwa mtu yeyote juu ya kosa au uachaji wa taarifa yoyote au kukosea kutaja kifungu cha sheria au sheria yenyewe katika chapisho hili. Mchapishaji na Mwandishi atawajibika tu ikiwa **TAARIFA** ya madai hayo yatawasilishwa kwao kwa njia ya maandishi ndani ya siku Saba (7) kwa ajili tu ya masahihisho, marekebisho na maboresho ya matoleo yajayo.